City Trees

City Trees

ID Guide to Urban and Suburban Species

Kenneth J. Schoon

STACKPOLE
BOOKS

Copyright © 2011 by Stackpole Books

Published by
STACKPOLE BOOKS
5067 Ritter Road
Mechanicsburg, PA 17055
www.stackpolebooks.com

Printed in the United States of America

Cover design by Caroline Stover.

10 9 8 7 6 5 4 3 2 1

First edition

Library of Congress Cataloging-in-Publication Data

Schoon, Kenneth J.
  City trees : an ID guide to urban and suburban species / Kenneth Schoon. — 1st ed.
    p. cm.
  Includes bibliographical references and index.
  ISBN 978-0-8117-0759-6
  1. Trees in cities. 2. Trees—Identification. I. Title.
  SB436.S35 2011
  635.9'77—dc22
                                2011000181

Contents

Acknowledgments

I am grateful to the following people for help in compiling and producing this book: Dianne Cutler, grounds supervisor at Indiana University Northwest; John Bachmann, grounds supervisor at Purdue University Calumet; Jim Hitz, Executive Director at Taltree Arboretum and Gardens, Indiana; Tom Allen, owner, and Lois Welch, of Allen Landscape, in Highland, Indiana; professional forester Gina Darnell; botanist Naida Lehmann; Ann Allen, Public Works Office Manager at Valparaiso, Indiana; Michelle Buckstrup Sutton, editor of *City Trees* magazine; John Chupek, Operations Manager, and Michael Mather, Board Certified Master Arborist, Urban Forestry Division, Richmond, Virginia; Brighton West, Friends of Trees at Portland, Oregon; photographers Beth Koebel, MD, and David Cappaert; Anne Koehler, Head of System Services, Indiana University Northwest Library; Aaron Pigors, Instructional Media Center at Indiana University Northwest; and several dozen others whose names I don't know who helped me access tree inventories of various communities. It was through these tree censuses that I was able to determine which trees are common in urban and suburban communities across the Midwest and northeastern portions of North America. I am especially grateful to Peg Schoon, a librarian and my wife of 40 years, who found much of the information in the third section and proofread the manuscript several times.

Introduction

A tree is a plant that grows to a height of at least 10 feet and has, from top to bottom, a crown of branches and leaves, generally one trunk several inches in diameter, and roots. Several tree species may grow to heights of over 100 feet.

Leaves are the food factories of the tree. It is in the leaves that water and minerals brought up from the ground and carbon dioxide from the air are converted (with the aid of sunlight) into sugary sap (the tree's food) and oxygen, which is then released into the air. The chemical that makes this happen, chlorophyll, is also what makes leaves green. Leaves come in many different sizes and shapes, and although most are green, some may be red or purple or even appear blue. Different species of trees have differently shaped leaves—a fact that is very useful in tree identification.

The trunk supports the upper part of the tree in two important ways. Most obvious is that it physically holds up the branches. But support also comes in the form of transportation. Within the trunk are structures called xylem, which transports water and dissolved minerals from the roots to the leaves, and phloem (also called the inner bark), which transports the sap downward to the roots. Surrounding the trunk is the tough outer bark, which protects the inner structures.

Roots usually spread in all directions from the trunk and hold the tree to the soil. Some trees have a large, long taproot that grows straight downward (just as a trunk grows upward). These trees are hard to dig up and transplant and so are not usually sold at landscaping centers. Other tree roots do not go directly downward but instead spread out in all directions rather close to the surface (these surface roots can cause nearby sidewalks to buckle). Roots, of course, provide the tree with water and minerals, which are absorbed by tiny root hairs at the ends of the roots. Roots serve another function: On sloping surfaces such as hills or steep slopes near rivers or ditches, roots cling to the soil and help prevent erosion.

Types of Trees

Evergreen trees are well known—they are the trees that bear living leaves (sometimes needles) year-round. Evergreen trees do drop their leaves, but new ones are formed before the old ones fall. Deciduous trees are those that drop their leaves every year. They are bare in winter and grow new leaves each spring. Conifers are those whose seeds are formed in cones and whose leaves are either needles (like pine trees) or overlapping scales (like arborvitae). Most conifers are evergreen—but not all. The baldcypress is a conifer with needles that turn brown and fall from the tree every autumn. It looks like an evergreen in the summer but not in the winter.

The Urban Forest

It is in cities and suburban communities that most people today have their first experiences with trees. It is here that kids first learn about nature and are fascinated by falling maple seed "helicopters." It is here that they learn about seasons by noting when new leaves form and old leaves fall, and it is here that they collect leaves for a school leaf collection. Older kids may earn spending money by raking leaves or help with the planting of new trees from a garden center.

The urban forest is quite different from the natural forests of North America. Trees in the natural forest are primarily native American trees (although a few nonnative trees have begun to infiltrate forests). The trees in a city are like the people in a city: They come from many different parts of the world. Although the city may contain, in places, remnants of a natural landscape, with the original forest trees still in place, most of the urban forest is the direct result of human planning and action. Most urban trees arrive at their location on a truck.

These trees have certain desirable characteristics. For many years, the American elm was the tree of choice in midwestern and northeastern cities. It grew dependably into a healthy, beautiful shade tree with a vaselike shape. Elms remained America's dominant city tree until the mid-1900s, when they were largely destroyed by Dutch elm disease. Another common city tree today, the silver maple, is a relatively inexpensive, fast-growing tree that also grows to a good size. For many decades now, silver maples have been planted in cities, especially in brand-new, treeless neighborhoods, because they can, within a few years, turn a bare street into a pleasant, semi-wooded one.

Smaller ornamental trees make up a big part of the urban forest. Magnolias, flowering pears, and crabapples welcome each spring with an abundance of white and pink flowers. Their smaller size works well with landscape designs for yards and in islands in parking lots. Other trees, including the honeylocust, weeping willow, and ginkgo, with their distinctive shapes, are chosen because they add visual interest to streetscapes. Oak trees may be chosen because they hold onto a portion of their leaves through much of the winter. Evergreen trees are often chosen because their color is maintained all year.

Urban forests do include some trees that grow quite naturally from seeds after the streets and yards are developed. These unplanned trees include many of those found along highways, rail lines, and alleys.

The Value of Trees

Trees serve many functions in urban areas. They can be beautiful and thus raise the property value of a residential lot. They soften the monotony of identical-looking commercial buildings, strip malls, or houses. They reduce air pollution and muffle the noise of busy highways. They remove carbon dioxide and freshen the air with oxygen. Their shade and the evaporation of water from their leaves cool the city on hot days. When deciduous trees are planted on the sunny side of a house, their summer shade can lessen the need for air conditioning and thus lower electric bills. In winter, the trees don't block the sunlight, which can then warm the house.

Simply put, trees in a neighborhood make that place a nicer and healthier place to live, as well as a more pleasant place to go for a walk.

Tree Names

All trees have at least two names: one or more common names and a scientific name (Latin or at least "Latinized"). The common name for a tree may differ from one country to another or even from one region of a country to another. For example, what English speakers call cottonwood may be called *alamo* by Spanish speakers. When a common name has two parts (such as silver maple) the first word names a subgroup of the second. The first common name often reflects a feature of the tree (red maple, quaking aspen) or may note where it originated (Norway spruce, Austrian pine).

Because of the confusion that can come from having different names for the same species of tree, the worldwide scientific community has established official scientific names for each species. The scientific name also has two parts, and in this case the group name (the genus) always comes before the individual name (the species). Thus *Populus deltoides* is the scientific name of the cottonwood no matter what language you speak.

All trees that are closely related to each other belong to the same genus (group) and thus have the same genus name. Scientific names are always written in italics, and the genus name is always capitalized. Many of the genus names are the actual ancient Latin words for those trees. For instance *Malus, Quercus, Pinus,* and *Fraxinus* are the Latin names for apple, oak, pine, and ash. Many of the species names are descriptive, such as *alba,* meaning "white," or *pennsylvanica,* meaning "of Pennsylvania." Thus the scientific name for white oak is *Quercus alba,* while the name for green ash is *Fraxinus pennsylvanica.* (In most cases, the common and scientific are not direct translations of each other.)

Of course, different tree species look different from each other. However, there are also slight differences within the species themselves. Not all people look exactly the same (even though we are all *Homo sapiens*) and not all red maples trees look exactly the same (even though they are all *Acer rubrum*).

Cultivars are "cultivated varieties," or subgroups of species deliberately bred to maintain some particular characteristic. Some cultivars are more resistant to cold weather, have especially large or beautiful flowers, grow in a particular way, have particularly colorful leaves, have no thorns, and so on. Cultivars have specific names, which are indicated by single quotation marks. An example is the 'Crimson King' Norway maple. Many cultivars are propagated through cuttings taken from trees. These cultivars are therefore clones of the original.

How many cultivars are there? No one knows. There are more than 600 cultivars of the crabapple alone. Before someone can finish making a complete list of cultivars someone else has developed a new one.

Most of the trees sold at landscape centers today are cultivars. You can buy a 'Crimson King' Norway maple, a 'Chanticleer' callery pear, or a 'Tri-Color' European beech. When you purchase a cultivar, you can have a good idea of what the tree will look like as it matures. For instance a 'Chanticleer' callery pear will have a taller and narrower growth habit than does the 'Aristocrat' callery pear, and so it is the better cultivar to place in a side yard between two houses.

The huge number of tree cultivars may cause confusion and sometimes makes identification of trees more complicated, but it certainly makes for a more interesting, healthy, and beautiful landscape.

Plant Hardiness

Many factors determine whether a tree species will thrive in a particular area. Among them are average yearly minimum and maximum temperatures, amount of sunlight, rainfall, elevation, humidity, soil dampness, air pollution, salt spray, soil acidity, and type of soil.

Of these, the one that is most often quantified is average yearly minimum temperature. In the 1950s, the United States Department of Agriculture determined that the ability of landscape plants to survive through winter was the most critical criterion in their being able to grow and thrive in an environment. Thus the United States and Canada were divided into zones showing the typical coldest temperatures of the year. Each zone has a minimum temperature 10 degrees Fahrenheit warmer than the zone to the north of

Zone	Average Minimum Temperature
1	Colder than -50
2	-50 to -40
3	-40 to -30
4	-30 to -20
5	-20 to -10
6	-10 to 0
7	0 to 10
8	10 to 20
9	20 to 30
10	30 to 40
11	40 and up

Key for hardiness zone map.

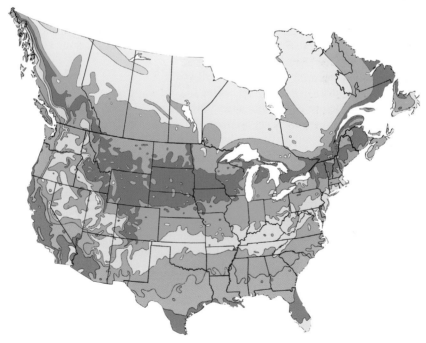

The USDA's plant hardiness zone map.

it. The first hardiness zone map was published in 1960. It was revised in 1965 and again in 1990.

Different species of trees can withstand differing extremes of cold weather and so may be hardy within specific zones. For instance, the white spruce *(Picea glauca)* is very tolerant of cold—hardy from zones 2 to 6. The sweetgum tree *(Liquidambar styraciflua)* is less tolerant of cold weather. It is hardy in zones 5 to 9. Possibly the biggest problem with the concept of the hardiness zone map is that it does not take into account the amount of summer heat. The hardiness figures in this book are primarily those published in 1998 by horticulturalist Michael A. Dirr.

Collecting Leaves

Making a leaf collection is a great way to get to know the trees in your neighborhood. Start with the trees closest to your home, school, or place of business. Do your collecting on public property, such as in parks and on public parkways along streets. Do not go into private yards without permission. Take along a small supply of paper that can be folded to make "L-velopes" (paper folded in half widthwise and taped closed along one edge), into which you can put the leaves and on which you can make notes. If possible, carry a camera to take pictures of the tree.

Before you remove a leaf from a tree, write down where the tree is located ("in front of 652 McKinley Street" or "north of the library") so that you can return to look again at that same tree later. Also note all interesting or unusual characteristics of the tree: whether there are any thorns or fruits on it, whether it has unusual bark, whether it is short or tall, and so on.

Determine what kind of leaves the tree has: simple, compound, needles, or scales. Leaves come in many shapes. Some are simple and have no lobes—they consist of a single blade with no projection that sticks way out from the main part of the leaf (although they may be serrated, with toothed edges like a serrated knife). Some leaves are simple with lobes. Others are

Simple leaf.

Simple leaf with lobes.

Pinnately compound leaf.

compound—they have several separate blades, called leaflets, on a single stalk. Pinnately compound leaves have leaflets arranged in a linear fashion, somewhat like a feather. Palmately compound leaves have leaflets that radiate in 5 or more directions from the base of the leaf—much as your fingers "radiate" from the palm of your hand.

Other leaves are needles or tiny scales. Scales and needles are usually found on "evergreen" trees, but not all trees with needles keep them all year. Scales are tiny. They are best seen with a magnifying glass.

Sometimes it's difficult to tell if a blade is a simple leaf or just one part of a compound leaf. One way to tell is to remove the blade from the tree. A leaf snaps off cleanly when it is broken off at its base. A leaflet does not. You have to tear the leaflet off the stem. Secondly, one can often see a bud (which will become the next year's leaf) at the base of a leafstalk but never at the base of the stem of a leaflet.

Finally, write down whether the leaves are aligned in an alternate, opposite, or whorled pattern on the twigs. It is important to make this note while you are still at the tree, because once the leaf is removed from the twig, you can't tell which arrangement it had.

Now find two clean, whole (not eaten by insects), healthy (not browned), and typical leaves on the tree and carefully remove both of them and place them in your L-velope with the notes written on it. If the tree has a variety of shapes of leaves (such as on mulberry or sassafras trees), take one or two of each.

Pressing leaves is a great way to preserve them. Leaves must be firmly pressed while they dry or they will wrinkle. The easiest way to do this is to place them on a smooth, flat, dry surface and cover them with a heavy, flat weight (such as a stack of heavy books) as soon as possible after collecting. It is best not

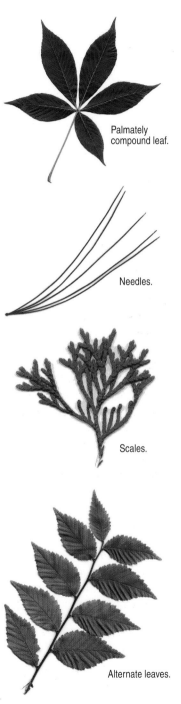

Palmately compound leaf.

Needles.

Scales.

Alternate leaves.

Collecting Leaves *continued*

to lay leaves on top of each other. Leave them under the weight for four or five days, and the leaves will be ready to mount.

Pressed leaves can be mounted for display in several ways. The easiest is to place them under the clear plastic covers of photo album pages. They can also be laminated or pasted onto paper or poster board. The leaves should then be identified with both their common and scientific names.

Opposite leaves.

Whorled leaves.

Identifying Trees

This book can help you find the names of the trees in your neighborhood or nearby park. All this requires is careful observation and reading of tree descriptions. It's important to first be familiar with the names of the various parts of the leaf.

To identify a tree species, first determine what type of leaf you have (simple without lobes, simple with one or more lobes, compound, needle, or scale). Then note whether the leaf has an opposite, alternate, or whorled arrangement, and whether it has a smooth margin or is serrated. Then, find the pages in this guide that describe the leaf.

Fickle Flowers and Fruits

Flowers and fruits can help identify trees, but, unfortunately, they are not always present on the tree, even during the growing season. In fact, trees don't even begin to have flowers or fruits until they are mature; for some trees, such as oaks, it might be 50 years before this happens. Nevertheless, when they are present, flowers and fruits can be very helpful, especially when the leaves aren't enough to make a positive identification.

Typical flower with 5 petals.

All tree species have flowers of some kind, but that isn't to say that all of them look like stereotypical flowers; they don't necessarily have brightly colored petals, stamens, and a pistil. In nature, not much seems to be typical. Some trees flowers are tiny and clustered in catkins that look somewhat like caterpillars. Sugar maple flowers have no petals at all.

"Double" flower with many petals.

Complicating the issue, some flowers (called perfect flowers) produce both pollen and seeds. Others are male, producing pollen but not seeds. Others are female, producing seeds but not pollen. Some species have separate male and female flowers on the same trees. Other species (such as ginkgo and boxelder) have them on separate trees. Some trees have flowers even when quite young. Others don't produce any flowers at all until they are quite old.

Flowers with no petals.

At best, flowers are only present for a few weeks, usually in the spring, and once they are gone they are of little help in identification. For a few years, a tree may have thousands of flowers, and then for several years afterwards it may have very few. At worst, you will look all year long and never see flowers on a particular tree.

Fruits contain the seeds of a tree. Like leaves, fruits (including cones) come in many sizes and shapes. Fortunately, at least when fruits are growing on trees, most tend to remain a lot longer than flowers do. Fruits begin to form

Flowers with tiny petals.

Fickle Flowers and Fruits *continued*

soon after the flowers are fertilized. While a few fruits, such as the "helicopters" or "keys" on the silver maple, mature within a few weeks and then drop, many others take months to grow before they ripen. Some fruits, such as those on sweetgum and many hawthorns, remain on the trees into the winter.

In many cases, the fruit on a tree can positively identify a tree. Red and black oak leaves are similar, but their acorns are quite different. So it's helpful when you find a tree with the fruits still on it.

Pollen cones.

Catkins.

Leaf Scars

On occasion, after examining leaves, flowers, and fruits, it is still difficult to distinguish between two related trees. Looking closely at leaf scars will help.

When a leaf is snapped off a twig, it leaves a leaf scar on the surface of the twig. The shapes and patterns of these scars are often used to identify trees, especially in winter. Leaf scars are not necessary to identify the trees in this book with one major exception: green and white ash. These two trees leaves are so close in shape to each other that observing the leaf scar is often the only way to tell the trees apart. On both trees, the leaf scar is immediately below a bud that will be the next year's leaf. The white ash scar looks like a C on its side, while the green ash scar is wider and looks more like a D on its side.

ID GUIDE

1. Trees with Leaves that are Needles or Scales

2. Trees with Simple, Unlobed Leaves

3. Trees with Simple, Lobed Leaves

4. Trees with Compound Leaves

5. Trees with Red or Purple Summer Leaves

CHAPTER 1

Trees with Leaves that are Needles or Scales

Eastern White Pine
Pinus strobus

Needles are up to 5 inches long, soft to the touch, flexible, and in clusters of 5.

Cones are long and narrow, from 3 to 8 inches long.

Eastern white pine may grow to a height of 50 to 80 feet.

Western White Pine
Pinus monticola

Similar to eastern white pine but with shorter needles (up to 4 inches long). The cones are longer (up to 10 inches long). The tree is commonly found from British Columbia to Colorado.

PINE TREES

Pines are easily recognized as a group because their needles are attached in clusters. Mature trees have pollen cones (shown here) that appear in spring. The seed cones are brown, usually egg shaped, and made of woody scales that are closed as the seeds mature then open to release them.

Loblolly Pine
Pinus taeda

Needles are yellowish green, in clusters of 3 (occasionally 2), and 6 to 10 inches long. Cones are 3 to 6 inches long.

Loblolly pine is a southern tree and grows to a height of 60 to 90 feet.

Ponderosa Pine
Pinus ponderosa

Needles are similar to those of loblolly pine (in clusters of 3) but much shorter (up to 4 inches long). Cones may be up to 10 inches long.

Ponderosa pine is commonly found from the far West to the upper Midwest.

Black Pine/Austrian Pine
Pinus nigra

Needles are dark green, up to 6 inches long, stiff, very dense on the tree, and in clusters of 2. They do not break crisply when bent as red pine needles do.

Black pine grows to a height of 50 to 60 feet.

Red Pine
Pinus resinosa

Needles are dark green, up to 6½ inches long, slender, and in clusters of 2. They break crisply when bent.

Pollen cones are red, which gives the tree its name.

Red pine grows to a height of 50 to 80 feet.

Scots Pine/Scotch Pine
Pinus sylvestris

Needles are blue-green, up to 3 inches long, and in clusters of 2.

The bark has splotches of orange-brown and may peel off in paperlike flakes.

Scots pine grows to a height of 30 to 60 feet.

The seed cones have stalks.

Jack Pine
Pinus banksiana

Needles are dark to grayish green, 1½ to 2 inches long, stiff, slightly flat, in clusters of 2, and often spread apart.

Cones are 1 to 1½ inches long and curve toward the end of the branch.

Jack pines grow to a height of 40 to 70 feet.

White Fir/Concolor Fir
Abies concolor

Bluish green needles are flat, about 1½ to 3 inches long, and occur in 2 rows on the branches. They curve outward and upward and have faint white lines made of stomata, or pores. When pinched, they give off a citrus smell.

Cones grow near the top of the tree. They are olive-green to purple, sit upright on the branches, are about 3 to 5 inches long, and disintegrate after the seeds are released.

White fir may grow to 150 feet.

Douglas-Fir
Pseudotsuga menziesii

Needles are flat, 1 to 1½ inches long, and soft to the touch. Unlike the white fir's, they stick out in all directions from the branch. Each needle has 2 faint white lines on the bottom side.

Cones are 3 to 4 inches long, hang down from the branches, and have 3-pointed bracts that stick out between the cone scales.

Douglas-fir grows as high as 130 feet.

SPRUCE, FIR, AND DOUGLAS-FIR
Spruce, fir, and Douglas-fir trees have conical shapes (especially when young) with evergreen needles not grouped in bunches. Spruce needles have 4 distinct sides; fir needles are flat. Spruce cones hang from the branches and fall when mature; fir cones sit upright on branches and disintegrate when mature.

Two Norway spruces behind a Colorado blue spruce.   White fir.

Colorado Spruce/Colorado Blue Spruce
Picea pungens

Needles are stiff, very sharp, and up to
1½ inches long, and range from bright
green to blue (when they are blue, the
tree's called a blue spruce).

Colorado spruce grows to 100 feet,
although some cultivars are dwarfs.

Cones are light brown, cylindrical,
and up to 3½ inches long. The cone
scales are thin with wavy edges. Each
scale has a tooth at its tip.

Norway Spruce
Picea abies

Needles are dark green, stiff, and ½ to
1 inch long. On larger trees, some
branchlets hang down from the larger
branches. Norway spruce grows to 125
feet.

Cones are brown, longer (up to 7
inches) than those of other spruces,
cylindrical, and slightly curved. The
scales are thin and stiff with a small
tooth at the tip.

White Spruce
Picea glauca

Needles are pale green or blue-green,
stiff, and ½ to ¾ inch long. Most needles grow on the upward side of the
branch. Branchlets do not hang down
from the branches as do those of the
Norway spruce.

White spruce grows to 75 feet.
Cones are brown, 1 to 2½ inches long,
and hang down from the branches. The
scales are thin and have rounded edges
with no teeth.

Yew

Taxus (species)

Evergreen needles are up to 1¼ inches long, flat, and soft, and grow in what appear to be 2 rows on a green twig. The needles have pointed tips and are tapered at the base.

Some yews may grow to 50 feet, but many are planted near buildings and trimmed to keep them short.

Inconspicuous male and female flowers grow on separate trees.

The seed cone (on female trees only) turns bright red, looking much like a berry when it ripens.

Eastern Hemlock/Canadian Hemlock

Tsuga canadensis

Evergreen needles are flat and up to ¾ inch long, and appear to be in rows of 2—except for a few needles that lie flat on the twig. Each needle has 2 bands of white on the bottom side. New-growth needles (shown here) are yellow-green; they later turn dark green.

Inconspicuous male and female flowers are yellow or green. Cones are light brown, small (to 1 inch), and hang down from the twig. Eastern hemlock often has a pyramid shape and may grow to a height of 70 feet.

Baldcypress
Taxodium distichum

Deciduous needles are flat, soft, and $\frac{1}{2}$ to $\frac{3}{4}$ inch long, and grow in 2 rows along a green shoot. Needles and shoots turn golden brown in autumn before falling.

Baldcypress may grow 50 to 70 feet high.

Inconspicuous male flowers droop from the branches in spring. Seed cones are round (like tiny soccer balls), up to 1 inch across, green to purple when immature, and brown when ripe.

Arborvitae/Northern White Cedar
Thuja occidentalis

Leaves are tiny green scales arranged in 4 rows around the twigs, which are usually arranged in upright, flat sprays. They are aromatic when crushed.

Arborvitae trees are often planted close in rows for screening. They can grow to a height of 50 feet.

Male flowers are small and yellow. Female flowers turn into rounded cones, which are leatherlike, not woody. Cones grow upright on the branches and occur in clusters (shown here). They are small (less than ½ inch) and green until they mature and turn brown.

Eastern Redcedar/Eastern Juniper
Juniperus virginiana

Leaves come in 2 shapes: Young trees have spreading, ¼-inch-long needles. Older tree leaves have tiny, greenish, overlapping scales, each about ⅛ inch long. They may smell like cedar chests when crushed.

The twigs are not in flat sprays as are arborvitae's. Leaves may turn slightly bronze in winter.

Eastern redcedar has a conical or pyramid shape when young. It can grow to a height of 40 to 50 feet.

Male and female flowers are usually on separate trees.

Seed cones (on female trees only) look like berries, are blue, ¼ inch across, with a thin, white wax cover (which can be rubbed off). Each cone contains 1 or 2 seeds. The bark is gray to reddish brown and peels off in long, narrow strips.

CHAPTER 2

Trees with Simple, Unlobed Leaves

Flowering Dogwood
Cornus florida

Leaves are opposite, oval but pointed at the tip, and up to 5 inches long, with smooth edges, veins that curve upwards toward the tip, and short ($^1/_2$ to $^3/_4$ inch) leafstalks.

Leaves turn red in autumn.

Flowering dogwood is a small tree (to 30 feet) with distinctive horizontal branches.

Flowers open before the leaves emerge. Tiny green "true" flowers grow in tight clusters surrounded by 4 showy white bracts up to 2 inches across.

The bright red, berrylike fruit, $^1/_4$ to $^1/_2$ inch long, occurs in small clusters and ripens in autumn.

Kousa Dogwood
Cornus kousa

Leaves are opposite, oval, and up to 4 inches long, with pointed tips and veins that curve upward toward the tip on short ($^1/_2$ to $^3/_4$ inch) leafstalks.

Leaves turn red to red-purple in autumn.

Kousa dogwood is a shrub or small tree and may grow as high as 20 or 30 feet. When young, its branches point upwards rather than horizontal as do the flowering dogwood's.

Flowers are similar to flowering dogwood's, but the bracts are narrower and tapered, and may be white or pink. They do not open until after the leaves do (about 2 to 3 weeks after the flowering dogwood's).

The bright red, raspberrylike fruit, $^1/_2$ to 1 inch in diameter, hangs on a 2-inch stem and ripens in late summer or autumn.

Simple, alternate or opposite leaves
with smooth margins and veins
that curve toward the tip

Alternate Leaf Dogwood/Pagoda Dogwood
Cornus alternifolia

Leaves are 2 to 5 inches long and similar to other dogwoods' (but are alternately rather than oppositely attached); they often cluster near the tip of the branch, however, and may appear opposite or whorled. The leafstalks, 1 to 2 inches long, are longer than the other dogwoods'.

The leaves may turn reddish or purple in autumn.

Flowers are unlike other dogwoods'—yellowish white, very fragrant, and forming flat-topped clusters at the ends of the branches. They bloom in late spring.

Fruits are berrylike ($1/4$ inch), bluish black, and hang on reddish stems. They ripen in midsummer.

Alternate leaf dogwood is a small tree (to 25 feet) with horizontal, spreading branches creating a layered look.

Japanese Tree Lilac
Syringa reticulata

Leaves are similar to the dogwoods': opposite, oval, and up to $5^{1}/_{2}$ inches long, with pointed tips, smooth edges, and veins curving upwards. The leafstalks may be up to 1 inch long.

No good fall color.

Twigs and bark have small, white, horizontal markings called lenticels.

Japanese tree lilac is a large shrub or small tree. It can grow to 30 feet high.

The flowers are showy, creamy white, and bunched on long (up to 12 inches) vertical stems (similar to a lilac bush's).

Fruits are small capsules borne on upright flower stems.

Star Magnolia
Magnolia stellata

Leaves are alternate, up to 4 inches long and about half as wide—but usually widest near the pointed tip—and tapered to the base; they have smooth, sometimes wavy, edges and short leafstalks.

Star magnolias are small trees (to 20 feet) and often have multiple stems like a shrub.

They are among the first ornamental city trees to bloom in spring. Flowers are white, fragrant, 3 to 4 inches across, with 12 to 18 long, narrow petals.

Fruits, if any, are reddish green, knobby aggregates about 2 inches long.

Saucer Magnolia
Magnolia soulangeana

Leaves similar to the star magnolia's but larger (up to 7 inches long), turning yellow in autumn.

Saucer magnolias are popular ornamental trees, found more often on residential lawns than along city streets.

Saucer magnolias are small (to 30 feet), often with low branches or multiple stems like a shrub.

The flowers are large and pink, purple, and/or white. They open before the leaves appear, usually a few days after the star magnolia blooms.

Fruits, if any, are 4-inch-long, knobby aggregates.

Pawpaw
Asimina triloba

Leaves are alternate, large (up to 12 inches long and 6 inches wide), not serrated, and tapered toward the base, with pointed tips and short (less than $^1/_2$ inch) leafstalks.

Pawpaw is a large shrub or mid- to small-sized tree with large leaves. It grows to 30 feet high.

Flowers are large (to $1^1/_2$ inches), brownish purple, and have a rancid odor.

Fruits are oval, green berries (to 5 inches) that turn blackish when ripened by mid fall.

Osage-Orange/Hedge Apple
Maclura pomifera

Leaves are alternate, egg shaped, tapered to the tip, bright to dark green on top, and up to 5 inches long, with a $^1/_2$- to $1^1/_2$-inch leafstalk.

Leaves turn yellow or yellow-green in autumn.

Twigs may have spines or thorns up to $^1/_2$ inch long. Several cultivars are sold today that have neither thorns nor fruits.

Flowers are inconspicuous.

Fruits, borne on female trees only, are yellowish, baseball-like aggregates (to 6 inches) that ripen in early autumn (and have a faint orange smell).

A midsize tree, osage-orange can grow to a height of 40 feet.

Common Persimmon
Diospyros virginiana

Leaves are alternate and oval, with a rounded base, pointed tip, and smooth margins. They range from 4 to 6 inches long and from 2 to 3 inches wide with a leafstalk up to 1 inch long.

Compare with blackgum.

Leaves turn yellow-green or reddish purple in autumn.

Bark on older trees is dark and chunky. The persimmon grows to 60 feet in height.

Male and female flowers typically grow on separate trees; they are white or greenish white and fragrant. Male flowers are often in groups of 3; female flowers grow singly.

The fruit (on female trees only) is a round, soft, generally orange ball (like a small tomato) about 1^1/$_2$ inches in diameter. Each fruit has several seeds.

Shingle Oak/Laurel Oak
Quercus imbricaria

Leaves are alternate, long (up to 10 inches), and narrow, shiny on the top side, with slightly wavy edges and a single, tiny bristle at the tip that shows the tree belongs to the red oak group. Leafstalks are ^{1}/$_4$ to ^{3}/$_4$ inch long.

Leaves turn golden brown to reddish brown in autumn. Many may remain on the tree into winter.

Shingle oaks grow as high as 60 feet.

Flowers are in yellow-green catkins that hang from the branches.

The fruit is a small, almost spherical, acorn ^{1}/$_2$ inch in diameter; the cap covers half the nut.

The acorns take 2 years to mature; they cling to the twigs during winter.

Black Tupelo/Blackgum
Nyssa sylvatica

Leaves are alternate, shiny, oval, and 3 to 7 inches long and 1 to 3 inches wide, with smooth margins and a $^1/_2$- to 1-inch leafstalk.

Similar to persimmon but has leaves clustered on short spurs of branches while the persimmon's are more evenly spaced on longer branches.

Spectacular color in autumn as leaves turn yellow, orange, scarlet, or purple.

Small, greenish flowers appear in spring. Male and female flowers are typically on separate trees.

Blueberrylike fruits ($^3/_8$ to $^3/_4$ inch)—only on trees that have female flowers—occur singly or in groups of 2 or 3. Fruits ripen in early autumn.

Black tupelo trees normally grow to a height of 30 to 50 feet.

Common Smoketree/'Royal Purple' Smoketree
Cotinus coggygria/Cotinus coggygria 'Royal Purple'

Leaves are alternate, oval, and up to $3^1/_2$ inches long, and have smooth margins and a leafstalk about $1^1/_2$ inches long. The leaves smell somewhat like orange peel when crushed.

Leaf color is commonly blue-green but can be dark purple or almost black on cultivars such as 'Royal Purple' (shown here). The dark leaves may have red stems and veins.

Leaves turn yellow, red, or purple in autumn.

Small, almost inconspicuous, flowers, in clusters like those of lilacs, bloom in early summer. After blooming, the more spectacular show begins as hairs on the flower stalks give a smoky appearance to the plant.

The fruit is small ($^1/_4$ inch) and kidney shaped.

A small tree or shrub, the smoketree grows to 15 feet high. It may be multistemmed or trimmed like a tree.

Southern Catalpa/Common Catalpa
Catalpa bignonioides

Leaves are opposite (sometimes whorled, with 3 leaves attached together), rarely lobed or with a few teeth, and pear to heart shaped, with pointed tips and smooth edges, and large (up to 10 inches long); they give off a bad odor when crushed. Leafstalks are up to 6 inches long.

Veins at the base of the leaf are not palmate (do not radiate) as on eastern redbud.

Leaves may turn slightly yellowish or brown in autumn, or may simply fall before turning.

Flowers, white with yellow and purple spots, bloom in late spring in clusters up to 8 inches high. Fruits are string bean shaped and up to 24 inches long. They give the tree its nickname, "cigar tree."

Southern catalpa trees may grow to 30 to 40 feet high.

Northern Catalpa/Hardy Catalpa
Catalpa speciosa

Similar to southern catalpa except leaves are larger (up to 13 inches long) and odorless. Its flowers have more yellow and purple coloring than southern catalpa's, and it blooms about two weeks earlier.

Northern catalpa may grow as high as 60 feet.

Eastern Redbud
Cercis canadensis

Heart-shaped leaves are alternate, with pointed tips and smooth edges. Smaller than the catalpa's, they grow to 5 inches long and wide. Base has 5 to 9 radiating veins.

Leaves turn yellow in autumn. The cultivar 'Forest Pansy' has maroon summer leaves.

Redbud is a small to midsize tree, growing as high as 30 feet.

Its tiny, pink to red flowers are among the first to bloom in spring, appearing before the leaves emerge.

Fruits are flat pods (to 3½ inches) that turn brown in late summer. Each pod may contain several seeds.

Catalpa in bloom.

Redbud in bloom.

Russian Olive
Elaeagnus augustifolia

Leaves are alternate, up to 4 inches long, narrow, not serrated, and dull gray-green on top and gray or silver on the back. Leafstalk is about $1/4$ inch long.

Leaves turn brown in autumn.

Russian olive trees can often be recognized from a distance because of their grayish foliage.

Little yellowish flowers (less than $1/2$ inch) in late spring produce $1/2$-inch-long, elliptical, berrylike, yellow to brown fruits.

Russian olives are shrubs or short trees that may grow as high and wide as 20 feet.

Peach
Prunus persica

Leaves are alternate, dark green, 4 to 9 inches long, and narrow, with tiny sharp teeth.

Leaves are wider than weeping willow's, and the branches do not droop as the willow's do.

Leaves turn yellow in autumn.

Flowers open before the leaves; they may be white, pink, or even red.

Fruit is a peach with 1 large seed (pit) in each.

Peach trees are much smaller than willows, growing only to a height of 15 to 25 feet.

Black Willow
Salix nigra

Leaves are alternate, shiny green, 3 to 6 inches long, narrow, and often curved at the tip. They have tiny, sharp teeth and a leafstalk about $1/4$ inch long.

Leaves are wider than weeping willow's and rounded instead of pointed at the base (and the branches do not droop).

Leaves turn light yellow in autumn.

Black willows are mid-sized trees growing to a height of 40 to 60 feet. Flowers, which open as the leaves emerge, are borne in 2- to 3-inch-long catkins.

Male and female flowers grow on separate trees.

Fruits (on female trees only) are tiny ($1/16$ inch), dry capsules.

Weeping Willow/Golden Weeping Willow
Salix alba 'Vitellina'

Leaves are alternate, long (up to 5 inches), finely serrated, on short stems, very narrow, and pointed at both ends.

Branches and leaves hang downward, giving the tree its common name.

Willow leaves are sometimes thought to be compound—they are not. Note that the image here shows 5 leaves.

Leaves turn yellow in autumn.

Green flowers are on catkins (to 4 inches) in early spring. Male and female flowers grow on separate trees.

Fruits (on female trees only) are tiny ($1/16$ inch), dry capsules that open and release seeds that are attached to long, white hairs and distributed by the wind.

Weeping willows, with their drooping branches, are distinctive trees. They may grow to a height of 40 to 80 feet.

American Beech
Fagus grandifolia

Leaves are alternate, shiny, dark green, leathery, oval but tapered, and up to 6 inches long, with 9 to 18 pairs of straight, parallel side veins. They are serrated with 1 tooth per vein and very short leafstalks. Leaf buds (about $3/4$ inch) are pointed and very prominent at the base of many of the leafstalks by early summer. The woody stems often have a zigzag pattern.

Leaf base is not lopsided like the American elm's [page 31]. Margins are not double toothed like the American elm's or either of the hornbeams'.

Leaves turn yellow, gold, orange, or bronze in autumn.

Bark is pale and smooth.

Flowers are not showy and bloom as the new leaves emerge. Males' are in $3/4$-inch, globelike clusters; females' grow in small clusters of 2 to 4.

Fruits are small (less than $3/4$ inch) nuts—beechnuts—inside reddish brown, spiny husks that split into 4 parts when ripe.

American beech trees may reach a height of 70 feet.

European Beech/Purple Beech/Tri-Color Beech
Fagus sylvatica/Fagus sylvatica 'Riversii' and 'Tri-Color'

Leaves are alternate and oval and smaller (up to 4 inches), less tapered, and with fewer pairs of veins (5 to 9) than American beech's. The leafstalk may be up to $1/2$ inch. The leaves may have smooth or wavy edges or irregular teeth. Leaf buds may be very prominent at the base of the leafstalks by early summer. Leaves are slow to emerge in spring.

Depending on the cultivar, leaves may be green or purple, or even bi- or tricolored.

European beech trees grow to a height of 60 feet.

Shown here are the cultivars 'Riversii,' the most common purple beech (which becomes greenish purple by late summer), and 'Tri-Color,' which has a variegated pattern. The cultivar 'Asplenifolia,' called cutleaf beech, has fernlike leaves.

Flowers are similar to American beech's. Fruit is a nut contained in a 1-inch, bristled, 4-lobed husk.

American Hornbeam/Blue Beech/Ironwood
Carpinus caroliniana

Leaves are alternate, 2 to 5 inches long, and 1 to 2 inches wide, with double-toothed margins and straight, parallel side veins that are seldom forked. The larger teeth are at the ends of the veins. Leaves have a rounded base and taper to a sharp point.

Leaves turn orange and scarlet in autumn.

Because its leaves look like beech leaves, the tree is also called "blue beech." Beech leaves are not double toothed, however.

American hornbeam grows to about 35 feet high.

Flowers, in $1^1/2$-inch catkins, bloom when the leaves appear in spring. Seeds are enclosed in light green three-pointed, leaflike "bracts" that grow in clusters on the branches.

The tree has a unique-looking thin, grayish trunk with a rather muscular appearance, giving the tree the nicknames "ironwood" and "musclewood."

Eastern Hophornbeam/Eastern Hornbeam
Ostrya virginiana

Leaves are alternate and oval, 3 to 5 inches long, with a pointed tip and rounded (sometimes heart-shaped) base, double-toothed margins, and parallel side veins that are often forked.

Leaves turn a dull yellow in autumn.

The bark is grayish brown and easily separates into short strips that may be loose at both ends.

Hophornbeam grows to a height of 25 to 40 feet.

Male flowers (catkins) appear in groups of 3 (to 1 inch) and persist through winter. Female flowers, $1/2$ inch long and light green, appear in spring.

Seeds are enclosed in flattened sacs (resembling hops) that occur in clusters that hang on hairy stems.

As is the American hornbeam, this tree is sometimes called "ironwood" because of its very hard, dense wood.

Chinkapin Oak
Quercus muehlenbergii

Leaves are alternate, dark green, oblong, and 4 to 7 inches long, and have coarse, bluntly pointed teeth with 1 tooth per vein. The leafstalk is $3/4$ to $1^1/2$ inches long.

Unlike most other oaks, chinkapin oak does not have lobes (but it has acorns, which makes it an oak).

Leaves turn yellow-orange to brownish orange in fall.

Chinkapin oak grows to a height of 50 feet.

Flowers appear in spring and are similar to those on other oak trees.

Seeds are $3/4$- to 1-inch acorns with cup-shaped lids that cover less than half the nut.

Japanese Zelkova
Zelkova serrata

Leaves are alternate and $1^1/2$ to 4 inches long, with short leafstalks, fairly straight, parallel veins, and serrated margins with rounded teeth.

Leaves turn yellow, orange, or copper in autumn.

Japanese zelkova grows to 50 to 80 feet high. It often has a handsome vase shape like that of the American elm (page 31).

Flowers are yellow-green and inconspicuous.

Fruits are oval and hard, about $1/2$ inch long.

Downy Serviceberry/Juneberry/Shadbush
Amelanchier arborea

Leaves are alternate, oval, 3 to 5 inches long, and finely serrated, with pointed tips and either rounded (as shown) or slightly heart-shaped bases on leafstalks up to $1^{1}/_{2}$ inches long.

Leaves turn deep yellow, red, or orange in autumn.

The bark is gray and smooth (sometimes slightly reddish). On older trees, it becomes rougher.

Clusters of showy white flowers (1 inch) appear in early spring.

Fruits are small ($^{1}/_{4}$ inch), round, dark red or purplish berries.

Serviceberries are shrubs or small trees growing 20 to 25 feet high, occasionally higher.

Cockspur Hawthorn
Crataegus crusgalli

Dark, glossy leaves are alternate, oval but tapered to the base, up to 4 inches long, and sharply serrated except near the base. The apex may be rounded (as shown) or pointed.

Leaves turn bronze-red to purplish red in autumn.

The branches have thorns 2 to 3 inches long.

Flowers, appearing in late spring, have 5 white petals $^{1}/_{2}$ to $^{3}/_{4}$ inch wide. They hang in clusters and have an unpleasant odor.

Fruits are red, oval, and about $^{1}/_{2}$ inch long.

Cockspur hawthorns may reach a height of 20 to 30 feet.

Common Buckthorn/European Buckthorn
Rhamnus cathartica

Leaves are sub-opposite, egg shaped, finely serrated, shiny, dark green, and up to 3 inches long. The bottom veins curve along the edge of the leaf.

Leaves remain green through mid autumn then turn yellowish green.

The tree has thorns and a crooked appearance and so is seldom used as a street or park tree.

Small, yellowish green flowers have 4 petals each and hang in clusters.

Berrylike fruits are small ($^{1}/_{4}$ inch) and shiny black.

Typically, buckthorn may grow as high as 25 feet.

Paper Birch/White Birch
Betula papyrifera

Leaves are alternate, up to 4 inches long, and coarsely serrated but not double toothed. They have 9 or fewer pairs of side veins, a pointed tip, and a rounded (or at least less sharply pointed) base.

Leaves turn yellow in autumn.

Bark on young trees is thin, smooth, and dark reddish brown. On older trees, it is white with thin, horizontal, black lines (lenticels) and often peeling or separating into papery layers—bright orange on the inner surface.

Paper birch grows to 80 feet in height. Its branches are upright and do not droop.

Separate male and female flowers grow on the same tree. The males grow in clusters of 1 to 3 catkins, about 1 inch long in winter, growing to 4 inches long when in bloom. Female flowers form in erect, greenish clusters (to $1\frac{1}{2}$ inches high).

Fruits are small nuts that form on caterpillarlike catkins (about 1 to $1\frac{1}{2}$ inches long) and ripen in early autumn.

River Birch
Betula nigra

Leaves are alternate, up to $3\frac{1}{2}$ inches long, medium to dark green, double toothed, and 4 sided, with a V-shaped, unserrated base on a short (less than $\frac{1}{2}$ inch), thin leafstalk.

Leaves turn golden-yellow to yellowish brown in autumn; they may drop quickly, however.

Bark is shaggy, peeling, or torn looking in shades of orange, brown, and black. The cultivar 'Heritage' has tan, cream, or parchment-white bark.

River birch may grow to a height of 75 feet.

Separate male and female flowers grow on the same tree. Males are catkins—$\frac{3}{4}$ inch long prior to blooming, 2 to 3 inches long in bloom, usually grouped in 3s. Female flowers are about $\frac{1}{2}$ inch long.

Fruits are similar to paper birch's but ripen in spring

European White Birch
Betula pendula

Leaves (up to 4 inches long) are 4 sided and taper to a point at the tip. The edges are irregularly double serrated.

Leaves turn yellow to yellow-green in autumn.

The bark is brown on young branches, changing to white with dark, horizontal bands (lenticels). It becomes darker with age and does not peel as much as paper birch's.

Smaller than the other birches, it grows to only about 50 feet high. Branches may droop as the tree gets taller. The trees are often planted in groups (called clumps).

Flowers, similar to paper birch's, form in clusters of 2 to 4. Fruits are also similar to paper birch's.

The European white birch is the most commonly planted birch in North America. It is highly variable with cultivars such as the purple-leaf birches; 'Golden Cloud,' with yellow leaves; 'Trista,' a weeping white birch with drooping branches; and 'Crispa,' a cutleaf weeping birch with highly dissected or fernlike leaves and weeping branches.

Purple-leaf White Birch
Betula pendula 'Purpurea,' *Betula pendula* 'Purple Rain,' *Betula pendula* 'Dark Prince'

Leaves are alternate, serrated or double serrated (except at the base), up to 4 inches long, and tapered to a sharp point. Flowers, fruits, and bark are the same as European white birch's.

'Purpurea' leaves are reddish purple in spring but gradually change to a bronze-green by late summer. 'Purple Rain' leaves keep their purple color longer than those of 'Purpurea.' 'Dark Prince' has dark purple leaves on somewhat weeping branches.

Other cultivars with purple leaves are less common.

American Basswood/American Linden
Tilia americana

Leaves are alternate, oval to heart shaped, 4 to 10 inches long and almost as wide, and sharply serrated, with irregular bases, a short pointed tip, and long (to 3 inches) leafstalks.

Leaves turn yellow to yellow-green in autumn.

Basswood trees grow to a height of 60 to 80 feet.

Flowers appear in late June to early July. They are small, fragrant, yellow, or white and appear in clusters hanging on long, leaflike bracts (shown here).

Fruits, also in clusters, are hard, round, and fuzzy.

Littleleaf Linden
Tilia cordata

Leaves are similar to but smaller than the basswood's. They are dark green, heart shaped, up to $3^1/2$ inches long, and sometimes wider than long, with irregular bases and a short pointed tip. They are sharply but finely serrated.

Leaves turn yellow to yellow-green in autumn.

The fragrant flowers and fruits are similar to basswood's. They are also attached to long, leaflike bracts.

Littleleaf linden may grow as high as 70 feet.

American Elm
Ulmus americana

Leaves are alternate, up to 6 inches long, and moderately rough to the touch (sometimes smooth), with parallel side veins (very few forked). They are double toothed (roughly alternating larger and smaller teeth) with lopsided bases and short leafstalk

Leaves turn yellow in autumn.

Mature trees typically have a vase shape with several large, symmetrical, upright limbs.

The flowers are greenish and inconspicuous. They appear in early spring.

The fruit, which matures in mid-to-late spring, is like a paper-thin, oval wafer, about $1/2$ inch long, with a notch at one end and a seed in the middle.

American elms grow to a height of 60 to 80 feet.

Slippery Elm/Red Elm
Ulmus rubra

Often confused with American elm, but its leaves are larger (up to 8 inches long) and rough, like sandpaper, on the top side. Several side veins may be forked. Its oval fruit is similar to American elm's but does not have a notch at either end.

Hackberry
Celtis occidentalis

Leaves are alternate, light to medium green, $2 1/2$ to 4 inches long, and single toothed (not double toothed like the American elm's). Also, unlike the elm's, hackberry leaves have 3 prominent main veins. The leaves also have rounded, unserrated, very lopsided bases. The tip tapers to a point that is usually slightly curved.

Leaves turn yellow-green or perhaps yellow in autumn.

The flowers are inconspicuous.

The fruit looks like a tiny, dark red to purple cherry, less than $1/2$ inch in diameter. It has a hard, round seed surrounded by a thin skin—with no soft flesh like a cherry.

Hackberry trees grow to a height of 40 to 60 feet.

Chinese Elm/Lacebark Elm
Ulmus parvifolia

Leaves are similar to the American elm's: alternate, with parallel side veins, slightly lopsided bases, and short leafstalks. They are smoother, however, not double toothed, and only 1 to $2^1/2$ inches long.

Leaf color in autumn is variable—sometimes red or yellow, sometimes still green even when the leaves fall.

Chinese elms may grow to a height of 40 to 50 feet.

Unlike on other elms, flowers appear in late summer. They are inconspicuous and often hidden by leaves.

The fruit is similar to American elm's but ripens in early autumn.

The distinctive bark is smooth and mottled brown mixed with green, gray, and orange.

Chinese elm is a desirable, tough, disease-resistant elm tree, but it's not as common in urban areas as the Siberian elm.

Siberian Elm
Ulmus pumila

Leaves are similar to the Chinese elm's, but the bases are not (or are at least less) lopsided. Like the American elm's, the leaves are slightly rough to the touch.

On many trees, most of the leaves have been eaten by insects by late summer.

Flowers and fruits are similar to the American elm's.

Many of these trees now in cities were planted in the 1930s and are tall and mature. The species is seldom planted today.

Siberian elm is a tough, disease-resistant elm tree, fast growing but messy, with weak, easily broken branches. It was, unfortunately, overplanted in past years.

Bigtooth Aspen
Populus grandidentata

Leaves are alternate, egg shaped to triangular, and 3 to 6 inches long, with large, conspicuous teeth. Leafstalks are flattened vertically and range in length from 1 to 3 inches.

Leaves turn yellow in autumn.

The bark is a distinctive gray—a bit greenish and smooth on young stems and grayish green and less smooth on older branches.

Flowers are in 3- to 4-inch-long, fuzzy catkins that appear before the leaves do. Male and female flowers grow on separate trees.

The fruit is composed of tiny capsules that hang in catkinlike clusters. Each capsule splits when mature and releases cottony seeds.

Bigtooth aspens grow to a height of 50 to 70 feet.

American Holly
Ilex opaca

Leaves are evergreen, alternate, $1\frac{1}{2}$ to $3\frac{1}{2}$ inches long, a bit like leather, and oval, with a few sharp teeth and short leafstalks. Compare with English holly.

Many hollies may grow as high as 50 feet, but most are trimmed as bushes.

Flowers are a dull white with 4 lobes.

The fruits are round, $\frac{1}{4}$ to $\frac{1}{2}$ inch, and bright red. Each contains tiny seeds.

English Holly/Meserve Hybrid Holly
Ilex aquifolium/Ilex x meserveae

Evergreen leaves are similar in size and shape to American holly's but are dark, shiny, green, and spinier. Some cultivars have leaves with white or yellow margins. Often trimmed as bushes, some cultivars grow as high as 12 feet.

Flowers and fruit are similar to American holly's.

Small branches of holly are often used to make wreaths and other holiday decorations.

Eastern Cottonwood
Populus deltoides

Leaves are alternate, roughly triangular or heart shaped, and coarsely toothed, up to 6 inches long and almost as wide. They are on long (up to 4 inches), flattened leafstalks.

The leaves flutter in light breezes and can be heard from a distance.

Leaves may turn yellow in autumn, but many fall while still green.

Cottonwood trees grow as high as 100 feet. They are seldom planted in cities but were often simply left standing, leftovers from days of yore.

Male and female catkins, 2 to 3 inches long, grow on separate trees and appear before the leaves.

Seeds grow in long clusters of small, green capsules. The tiny brown seeds with many long white hairs are then released and easily blown by the wind.

Quaking Aspen
Populus tremuloides

Leaves are alternate, roughly circular, 1 to 3 inches long and wide, shiny green, and finely serrated. Leafstalks, up to $2^1/_2$ inches long, are thin and flattened.

The leaves flutter even in light breezes, giving the tree its name.

Leaves turn bright or golden yellow in autumn.

Catkins are similar to the cottonwood's but are 4 to 5 inches long. Seeds are also like cottonwood's.

The bark on young aspens is smooth and cream colored; on older trees, it's rougher and darker.

Quaking aspens have trunks that are usually tall and straight. The trees may reach a height of 40 to 50 feet.

Black Alder
Alnus glutinosa

Leaves are alternate, oval to nearly circular, up to 4 inches long, blunt-tipped (sometimes notched), and coarsely double serrated, with straight side veins and a leafstalk $1/2$ to 1 inch long. Leaves are gummy when young.

Leaves remain green late into autumn before turning brown and falling.

Male and female flowers appear on the same tree. Male flowers are 2- to 4-inch, reddish brown catkins that hang in clusters of 3 to 5; female's are purplish and much shorter.

Fruits are "cones" on long ($1/2$ to $7/8$ inch), slender stems.

Black alders grow to 60 feet high.

Katsuratree
Cercidiphyllum japonicum

Leaves are opposite on the branch, 2 to $3^1/2$ inches long, heart shaped, and serrated, with blunt teeth. The leafstalk is $3/4$ to $1^1/2$ inches long. The veins at the base of the leaf are palmate.

New leaves are reddish purple at first, changing to green; they turn yellow-orange in autumn and then give off a spicy odor somewhat like brown sugar.

Small, greenish, not showy flowers open before the leaves do. Male and female flowers grow on separate trees.

The fruit (on female trees only) is a short ($3/4$ inch) pod, like a pea pod. Pods are usually in groups of 2 to 4 and have small, winged seeds inside.

Katsuratrees may grow to a height of 60 feet.

Apple/Orchard Apple/Common Apple
Malus x domestica

Leaves are alternate, oval, up to 3 inches long, and serrated, with a pointed tip and, sometimes, a heart-shaped base.

Apple is a small tree, growing to a height of 20 to 30 feet. It is more often found in backyards than on public property. In summer, this tree is easily identified by its fruit.

Flowers are white to pink, have 5 petals, and are up to $1^1/_2$ inches across.

Fruits are the familiar apples, yellow or red and sunken at both ends. The star-shaped core has 10 or more seeds.

Callery Pear
Pyrus calleryana

Leaves are alternate, oval to heart shaped, up to 3 inches long, and shiny green on top and pale green on the back, with finely toothed edges, a pointed tip, and a leafstalk 1 to $1^1/_2$ inches long.

Leaves turn yellow, orange, and/or red in autumn.

Callery pear is a midsize tree growing to a height of 35 feet.

Flowers are showy, $^1/_2$ to $^3/_4$ inch across, with 5 white petals. They appear in 2- to 4-inch clusters before or as the leaves emerge.

Fruit is small ($^1/_2$ inch), round, and green to tan. It is not edible as are fresh pears.

FLOWERING FRUIT TREES
Many of the flowering fruit trees included here have similar alternate, roughly oval, serrated leaves. Whereas flowers can be useful in identifying trees, they are visible only a few weeks a year. The fruits (crabapples, pears, cherries, and so on) are often more useful in tree identification because they are visible much of the summer.

Crabapple
Malus (species)

Crabapples are quite variable, with some 600 cultivars and more being introduced each year. All are short, reaching a height of just 15 to 25 feet, but the color of the leaves and fruits differs. Some trees have thorns.

Leaves are alternate, roughly oval, up to 3 inches long, and serrated. The tip is pointed, as is the base, but it may also be heart shaped. Some leaves may have a couple large teeth (almost lobes) near the base.

Summer leaves may be green, green with red mottling, red, orange, greenish purple, or dark purple.

Showy spring flowers are white to pink to dark rose, have 5 petals, and are up to $1^1/_2$ inches across. Some trees have "double flowers" with extra petals.

Fruits are red, orange, yellow, green, or even purple crabapples less than 2 inches in diameter, hanging on long stems, with tiny, oval, brown seeds.

Purple Leaf Plum
Prunus cerasifera

Leaves are alternate, oval, up to $2^1/2$ inches long, and finely serrated. They have a $^1/2$-inch-long leafstalk and may have a pointed tip.

The natural species' leaves are green, but those of the popular cultivars are purple. Shown here is the 'Newport' cultivar.

These small plum trees may grow to a height of 25 to 30 feet. Showy, fragrant, pink or white flowers have 5 petals, are 1 inch in diameter, and appear in early spring, before the leaves emerge.

Fruit is round, up to 1 inch in diameter, and red or purple with a stony pit.

Weeping Higan Cherry
Prunus subhirtella 'Pendula'

Dark green leaves are alternate, up to 4 inches long and $^1/2$ to 2 inches wide—wider than a weeping willow's—and finely toothed, some-times double toothed. The branches and leaves droop gracefully toward the ground, giving the tree its name.

Leaves turn yellow to orange in autumn.

Flowers bloom before the leaves appear in spring. They are found in groups of 2 to 5 and are pink to white, $^1/2$ inch in diameter. Some varieties have double flowers with overlapping petals.

Fruits are red to black, less than $^1/2$ inch in diameter, with 1 seed inside.

The weeping Higan cherry may attain a height of 20 to 30 feet.

Black Cherry
Prunus serotina

Leaves are alternate, up to 6 inches long, and sometimes narrow or oval, with blunt teeth and $1/4$- to 1-inch-long leafstalks. They have more than 13 pairs of lateral veins.

This tree is easily identified by its multiple fruit.

Bark on larger trunks is gray to black and scaly, with tiny, light lenticels.

Black cherry trees grow as high as 80 feet.

White flowers with 5 petals each hanging in clusters appear in spring.

The fruits, unlike the familiar red cherries, are small ($1/4$ inch) and red, turning purple or black when ripe. They hang in clusters from the twigs.

Japanese Flowering Cherry
Prunus serrulata/Prunus serrulata 'Kwanzan'

Leaves are alternate, oval but tapered toward the tip, 2 to 5 inches long, and sharply serrated, with a $1/2$- to 1-inch leafstalk.

Leaves turn bronze or slightly red in autumn.

Most cultivars grow to a height of 20 to 25 feet.

Showy white or pink flowers bloom in spring as the leaves begin to emerge. They are quite variable, ranging from $1/2$ to $2^{1}/2$ inches across and may be either single or double flowered (with up to 35 petals).

Fruits (if any) are cherries, each containing 1 pit.

'Kwanzan,' with its pink double flowers, is the most popular cultivar.

Ginkgo
Ginkgo biloba

Fan-shaped leaves are 2 to 5 inches wide with a leafstalk from $1^1/_2$ to 4 inches long. Veins fan out from the base to the top. Leaves have wavy top margins and are sometimes split near the middle.

Leaves turn bright yellow in autumn.

Ginkgo grows to a height of 60 to 80 feet.

Male and female flowers grow on separate trees (and may not appear at all until the tree is 40 years old). Male flowers are in 1-inch-long green catkins; females are on 2-inch-long stalks.

Fruits (on female trees only) are like yellow-orange plums, about 1 inch long. They ripen in late summer. Because the fruits smell bad, most nurseries sell only fruitless male ginkgoes.

CHAPTER 3

Trees with Simple, Lobed Leaves

Silver Maple
Acer saccharinum

Leaves are opposite, up to 6 inches across, and have 5 lobes with sharp teeth and long, smooth, V-shaped notches between them. Leaves are green on top and silver-green on the back, with a green leafstalk 3 to 5 inches long (compare with 'Autumn Blaze' maple).

Leaves turn yellow in autumn.

Silver maple may grow to a height of 70 feet or more.

Tiny flowers with no petals appear in very early spring.

Large ($1^1/_2$ to 3 inches), winged seeds, in pairs, ripen in spring.

Red Maple/Swamp Maple
Acer rubrum

Leaves are opposite, 2 to 4 inches long and wide, and have 3 to 5 lobes with sharp teeth and short (but variable), V-shaped notches between the lobes. Leafstalks, 2 to 4 inches long, are often red.

Leaves often turn bright red in autumn.

Red maple grows to a height of 60 feet.

Clusters of tiny, red (or sometimes yellow) flowers bloom in early spring, before the leaves appear.

Small (1 inch), often reddish, winged seeds, in closely spread pairs, hang in bunches on long stems. They ripen in spring.

Freeman Maple/"Autumn Blaze' Maple
Acer x freemanii 'Jeffersred'

A cross between silver and red maples, its leaves are similar to silver maple's but with red leafstalks. They turn brilliant red-orange in autumn. Seeds, if any, are similar to those of red maples.

Japanese Maple
Acer palmatum

Leaves are opposite, small (2 to 4 inches long and wide), and have 5 to 9 narrow, serrated, palmate lobes. They may be red or green, solid or dissected (both shown here). Leafstalk may be $3/4$ to 2 inches long.

Leaves turn red, yellow, orange, or purple in autumn.

Small, reddish flowers bloom when the leaves emerge.

Widely spread pairs of curved, winged seeds (less than 1 inch) ripen in autumn.

Japanese maple trees reach only a height of 8 to 25 feet, depending on the cultivar.

Sweetgum
Liquidambar styraciflua

Leaves are alternate, star shaped, and up to 5 to 7 inches long and wide, and have 5 (sometimes 7) long, tapered, finely serrated lobes. The leafstalk is $2^1/2$ to 4 inches long.

Leaves turn a rich combination of yellow, red, and purple in autumn.

Sweetgum trees grow to a height of 60 to 75 feet.

Inconspicuous flowers form as the leaves appear in spring.

Fruits are long-stemmed, dry, prickly, brown balls. They turn black and often remain on the tree through winter.

Sugar Maple
Acer saccharum

Leaves are opposite, up to 6 inches across, and coarsely toothed. They have 3 to 5 lobes with U-shaped sinuses between them and a $1^1/_2$- to 3-inch leafstalk.

Leaves are green (never purple), turning yellow or burnt-orange in autumn.

Compare with Norway maple and London planetree (page 46).

Sugar maple trees may grow to a height of 75 feet.

Tiny, green flowers with long stems and no petals open in spring before the leaves do.

The winged seeds (1 to $1^1/_2$ inches) are in slightly spread pairs and ripen in autumn.

Norway Maple
Acer platanoides

Leaves are opposite, up to 7 inches across, and coarsely toothed. They have 5 lobes with U-shaped sinuses between the lobes and a 3- to 4-inch leafstalk.

Leaves are similar to sugar maple's except that the leafstalks exude milky sap when removed from the stem and squeezed (this may not happen when dry).

'Crimson King' and some other cultivars have purple or maroon leaves.

Leaves turn yellow in autumn.

Tiny, yellow to greenish yellow flowers open in spring before the leaves emerge.

Winged seeds ($1^1/_2$ to 2 inches) occur in widely spread pairs and ripen in autumn.

Norway maples may grow to a height of 50 feet.

Hedge Maple
Acer campestre

Leaves are opposite and 2 to 4 inches long and wide, with 3 to 5 rounded lobes separated by U-shaped sinuses. The leafstalk may be up to 4 inches long and, like Norway maple's, exudes a milky sap when removed from the twig and squeezed.

Fall color is variable—yellow, orange, red, or purple.

Hedge maples typically grow to a height of 35 feet.

Flowers are small, green, and inconspicuous.

Hedge maple seeds (less than $1^{1}/_{2}$ inches) occur in very widely spaced pairs (about 180 to 185 degrees apart). They ripen in autumn.

Bigleaf Maple/Oregon Maple
Acer macrophyllum

The largest of all maple leaves, they are opposite, up to 22 inches across, and have 5 to 7 lobes with U-shaped sinuses and a 10- to 12-inch leafstalk that secretes a milky sap when removed from the twig and squeezed.

Leaves turn yellow-orange in autumn.

Bigleaf maple typically grows only within 200 miles of the Pacific Ocean. It grows to a height of 45 to 75 feet.

Fragrant, yellow flowers are borne in clusters up to $8^{1}/_{2}$ inches long; each flower may be $^{1}/_{4}$ inch across.

Winged seeds, $1^{1}/_{2}$ inches long, mature in autumn.

Simple leaves with palmate lobes and U-shaped sinuses

London Planetree
Platanus x acerifolia

Leaves are alternate, grow up to 9 inches wide, and have 3 to 5 shallow, roughly triangular lobes with large, pointed teeth. The leafstalks are long (to 4 inches) and have hollow bases. Compare with American sycamore and sugar and Norway maples (page 44).

Leaves turn brown in autumn.

The outer bark often flakes off, exposing mottled, multicolored inner bark. London planetrees can grow to a height of 75 to 100 feet.

Flowers are usually inconspicuous.

The fruit (1-inch balls called buttonballs) are surrounded by tiny bristles and hang (usually in pairs) on long, drooping stems.

American Sycamore/American Planetree
Platanus occidentalis

Leaves are similar to London planetree's except that the lobes are shallower and may look unlobed. The tree occurs in natural woodlands, seldom in landscaped city parks or along residential streets.

White Poplar
Populus alba/Populus alba 'Bolleana'

Leaves are alternate, grow up to 5 inches long, and have irregular lobes or wavy edges and a leafstalk up to $1^{1}/_{2}$ inches long. They are dark green on the front and white and fuzzy on the back.

Leaves often drop before color change in autumn.

Flowers are long (to 3 inches), drooping catkins. Male and female flowers grow on separate trees.

Fruits (on female trees only) are 2-valved capsules.

Amur Maple
Acer ginnala

Leaves are opposite, up to $3^1/_2$ inches long, and only $2^1/_2$ inches wide, with 3 double-serrated lobes and V-shaped notches between the lobes.

Unlike most other maples, amur maple leaves are distinctly longer than wide, the middle lobe being much longer than the side lobes.

Compare with Rose of Sharon.

Leaves turn yellow or red in autumn, depending on the cultivar.

Flowers are yellowish white and fragrant (few other maples have fragrant flowers).

Small (1 inch), winged seeds (sometimes red) in U-shaped pairs grow in clusters and ripen in summer.

Amur maple is a small tree, growing only as high as about 20 feet.

Rose of Sharon
Hibiscus syriacus

Leaves are alternate and up to 4 inches long, and have 3 lobes with coarse, rounded teeth. The leafstalk may be $^1/_4$ to 1 inch long.

Rose of Sharon is a shrub or small tree sometimes reaching a height of 10 to 12 feet. It has a vaselike shape with gray bark and upright, spreading branches.

Flowers appear in late summer when few other trees have blooms. The bright flowers, 2 to 4 inches across, may be red, white, light blue, or lavender and last for several weeks.

The fruit (if any) is a green to brown 5-part capsule that remains on the tree through winter. Many cultivars are seedless.

White Oak
Quercus alba

Leaves are alternate, up to 9 inches long, and dark green. They have 5 to 9 lobes with smooth edges and rounded tips. Notches between the lobes are long and rather even. The base of the leaf is pointed, and the leafstalk is $1/2$ to 1 inch long.

Leaves turn dark red or burgundy in autumn. After they turn brown, many of them may remain on the tree into winter.

The white oak grows to 100 feet high.

The acorn is set in a shallow cap (covering a third or less of the nut).

English Oak/Pedunculate Oak
Quercus robur

Small, alternate leaves (2 to 5 inches) have 7 to 11 shallow lobes with rounded tips and a very short leafstalk (about $1/4$ inch long). Unlike the white oak's, the base of the leaf is rounded, similar to the side lobes. Some cultivars have thick, leathery leaves.

The leaves turn yellow or brown in autumn, or may just fall while still green.

The fruit is an elongated acorn about 1 inch long, about a third to a half covered by the cap. The acorns hang in clusters of up to 5 on long (to 4 inches) stalks.

English oaks grow to a height of 40 to 60 feet.

Bur Oak
Quercus macrocarpa

Leaves are alternate and up to 12 inches long, and have 5 to 9 lobes with smooth edges and rounded tips. The leaves are clustered near the ends of the twigs. The top lobe is larger than the others, and the notch below it extends nearly to the mid vein. The leafstalk is up to 1¹/₄ inches long.

Leaves turn yellow or yellowish brown in autumn. Many remain on the tree into winter.

The acorn is set in a unique, large, fringed cap that covers at least half the nut.

Bur oaks grow to a height of 80 feet.

Swamp White Oak
Quercus bicolor

Leaves are alternate and up to 7 inches long, and have several of what could be called either "rounded lobes with smooth edges" or "large, rounded teeth." The leaf is always wider toward the tip than toward the base, which is pointed; the yellowish leafstalk is ¹/₂ to ³/₄ inch long.

Leaves turn yellow, dark red, or reddish purple in autumn. After they turn brown, many of them may remain on the tree into winter.

The acorn is oval, usually found in pairs and hanging on a long stem.

Swamp white oaks grow to a height of 70 feet.

OAK TREES
All mature oak trees in spring have male flowers—which are long, green catkins—and separate, smaller, female flowers that form acorns after fertilization. Some oaks don't reach maturity until they are 50 years old.

Red Oak/Northern Red Oak
Quercus rubra

Leaves are alternate, grow up to 8 inches long, and have 7 to 11 bristle-tipped lobes. Leafstalks are stout and may be up to 2 inches long.

Leaves turn red to brown in autumn. Many stay on the tree into winter.

Red oak reaches a height of 75 feet.

The acorn is set in a shallow, saucer-like cup.

Often confused with black oak—if planted in a park or lawn, it's most likely red oak.

Pin Oak
Quercus palustris

Leaves are alternate and up to 6 inches long, and have 5 to 7 deeply divided, skinny, bristle-tipped lobes with notches cut nearly to the center vein.

Leafstalks are thin and may be up to 2 inches long.

Leaves turn red or brown in autumn. Many stay on the tree into winter.

The acorn is short, round, often striped, and set in a shallow, saucerlike cup.

Pin oaks grow to a height of 70 feet.

Black Oak
Quercus velutina

Shiny, leathery-looking leaves are alternate and up to 10 inches long, and have 5 to 9 bristle-tipped lobes. Leafstalks are stout and may be up to $2^1/2$ inches long.

Leaves turn orange-brown in autumn. Many stay on the tree into winter.

Black oak reaches a height of 60 feet.

The fruit is an acorn set in a bowl-shaped cup that covers about half the acorn.

Black oak's long taproot makes it difficult to transplant. It's normally found in natural areas rather than parks or parkways.

English Hawthorn/Midland Hawthorn
Crataegus laevigata

Dark green leaves range from $1/2$ to $2^1/2$ inches long and have 3 to 5 serrated lobes and a short ($1/4$ to $3/4$ inch) leafstalk.

English Hawthorn is a short (to 20 feet), low-branching tree with thorny branches.

Flowers are white, about $1/2$ inch across, occurring in flat-topped clusters of 5 to 15 blooms.

Fruits are red or bright yellow, round, and about $1/2$ inch across. Each contains 2 to 3 seeds.

(There are more hawthorns on the following pages.)

Downy Hawthorn/Red Hawthorn
Crataegus mollis

Leaves are alternate, up to 5 inches long, and coarsely double toothed. They usually have a few pairs of shallow lobes and a 1- to 2-inch leafstalk.

Thorns, if present, may be 2 inches long.

Leaves turn yellow to reddish bronze in autumn.

Downy hawthorns may reach a height of about 30 feet.

Flowers are white, 1 inch wide, and appear in 3- to 4-inch flat-topped clusters. Downy hawthorn is among the first of the hawthorns to bloom in spring.

Fruits are red, $1/2$ to 1 inches in diameter, hang in clusters, and ripen in summer, falling soon afterward.

Green Hawthorn/'Winter King' Hawthorn
Crataegus viridis/Crataegus viridis 'Winter King'

Leaves are alternate, shiny, dark green, $1\frac{1}{2}$ to $3\frac{1}{2}$ inches long, serrated, and shallowly lobed. The leaf is roughly oval and not heart shaped, as the Washington hawthorn's sometimes is.

Leaves turn orange, red, or purple in autumn.

Branches may have sharp thorns up to $1\frac{1}{2}$ inches long. Green hawthorns grow to 20 to 35 feet high. Flowers are white, $3/4$ inch across, and appear in 2-inch-wide, flat-topped clusters.

Fruits are red, $1/4$ inch across, hang in clusters, and ripen in summer.

'Winter King' has larger fruits that usually persist on the tree into winter, giving it nice color as well as its name.

Washington Hawthorn
Crataegus phaenopyrum

Leaves are alternate, up to 3 inches long, shallowly lobed, and double serrated, and have a straight or roughly heart-shaped base.

Fall foliage ranges from orange to red.

The branches bear 1- to 3-inch thorns.

Washington hawthorns grow to a height of 25 to 35 feet.

Flowers are white, $1/2$ inch across, and in flat-topped clusters blooming in late spring.

The fruits are round, red, and less than $1/4$ inch in diameter. They hang from the branches in small clusters, often staying on the tree into winter.

Tuliptree/Yellow Poplar
Liriodendron tulipifera

Leaves are alternate, bright green, and up to 8 inches long and across, with 3 to 4 large lobes (the top 2 lobes sometimes appear as just one) and a 2- to 4-inch leafstalk.

The top of the leaf sometimes looks like it was cut off with scissors.

Leaves turn bright yellow in autumn.

The tuliptree may grow to a height of 90 feet (taller in the South).

Large, tulip-shaped flowers are up to 3 inches wide and have 6 orange, green, and yellow waxy petals. The flowers often grow only on upper branches and are hard to see.

Fruits are upright clusters of numerous seeds that drop from the tree in autumn and winter.

Sassafras
Sassafras albidum

Leaves are alternate and 4 to 7 inches long, and have smooth edges and leafstalks up to $1^1/2$ inches long. The leaves may be unlobed, have 2 lobes (like a mitten), or 3 lobes—all on the same tree.

Leaves turn red, orange, or purple in autumn.

Sassafras is a midsize tree that grows as high as 30 to 60 feet.

Flowers are small and yellow-green. They appear with the leaves in the spring.

Fruits are egg shaped, dark blue or black berries, each on a fleshy, bright red stalk.

White Mulberry
Morus alba

Leaves are alternate, 3 to $5^1/2$ inches long, and coarsley toothed, with leafstalks up to $1^1/2$ inches long. Their shape is quite variable: some may be heart shaped with no lobes, others may have 2, 3, 4, or more lobes—all on the same tree. Compare with red mulberry.

Leaves turn pale yellow in autumn.

The bark on new branches is smooth and yellow or tan; on older branches, it's rougher and brown.

Flowers are green and inconspicuous.

Fruits are pink to red to black (rarely white) "berries" composed of multiple sections (similar to blackberries). Each section contains a small seed.

White mulberries can grow as high as 30 to 50 feet. They are often found in alleys and other nonlandscaped areas.

Red Mulberry
Morus rubra

Red mulberry has leaves similar to white mulberry's except that they are larger (up to 10 inches long), darker, and not shiny, and have finely serrated margins. The tree grows in moist, shady, wooded locations and is not common in cities.

CHAPTER 4

Trees with Compound Leaves

Ohio Buckeye
Aesculus glabra

Leaves are opposite, up to 15 inches wide, and palmately compound, with 5 or 7 leaflets and long (up to 5 inches) leaf stems. Leaflets (up to 6 inches long) are oval, finely serrated, pointed at both ends, stemless, and widest near their centers. Leaflets give off a foul odor when crushed.

Leaves turn yellow, orange, or red in autumn.

Flowers, yellow-green and hairy, appear in spring on branch tips in large (up to 10 inches), upright clusters. Fruits are round, spiny husks (up to 2 inches) containing large brown seeds called buckeyes.

Ohio buckeye is a midsize tree, growing to a height of 60 feet.

Common Horsechestnut
Aesculus hippocastanum

Leaves (up to 20 inches wide) are opposite and palmately compound, with 5 to 9 leaflets and long (up to 7 inches) leaf stems. Leaflets are up to 10 inches long, oval, coarsely serrated, pointed at both ends, stemless, and widest near their outside ends.

Leaves turn yellow in autumn.

Flowers, white or cream colored, appear in late spring in large (up to 10 inches), upright clusters (compare to red horsechestnut). Fruits are round, spiny husks (up to $2^1/2$ inches) containing 1 or 2 large, rounded, shiny, brown seeds.

Common horsechestnut grows to a height of 75 feet.

Red Horsechestnut
Aesculus x carnea

Leaves and fruits are similar to but slightly smaller than common horsechestnut's. Flowers also similar but deep pink or red.

Compound leaves with many oval/pointed leaflets

Honeylocust
Gleditsia triacanthos

Compound leaves (up to 11 inches long) are alternate and may be both singular (bottom photo) and doubly (bipinnately) compound (top photo) on the same tree. Each stalk has an even number of leaflets, with no single leaflet at the tip. The numerous leaflets are small (up to 1 inch long), stemless, and oblong, with almost smooth, slightly toothed, or wavy edges.

Leaves are usually green, but the cultivar 'Sunburst' has bright yellow leaves in spring. Branches may have long thorns, but thornless varieties are widely available.

Honeylocust can grow to a height of 30 to 80 feet, depending on the cultivar.

Compare with black locust (page 61), whose leaflets have stems, and European mountain-ash (page 61), whose leaflets are sharply serrated.

Flowers are greenish yellow and grow in small clusters. They are fragrant but rather inconspicuous.

Fruits are flat, twisted, brownish pods up to 18 inches long, and contain several brown, flat seeds. Many cultivars are fruitless.

Kentucky Coffeetree
Gymnocladus dioicus

The Kentucky coffeetree has the largest leaves of any tree in eastern North America, up to 36 inches long. They are alternate and doubly (bipinnately) compound with up to 70 leaflets. The lower part of the leaf may have a few pairs of simple leaflets (1 to 3 inches), which are oval and have smooth edges and pointed tips.

Leaves turn yellow in the fall.

The Kentucky coffeetree may grow to a height of 100 feet.

The flowers are white and fragrant, with yellow spots, and bloom in mid to late spring in long (5 inches), drooping clusters. Male and female flowers grow on separate trees.

The fruits (on female trees only) are large, flat, brown pods, up to 10 inches long. Generally, only male trees are preferred for residential use.

Japanese Pagodatree/Chinese Scholar-tree
Sophora japonica

Leaves are alternate, grow up to 10 inches long, and have 7 to 17 teardrop-shaped leaflets with smooth margins.

The leaves may remain green in autumn or turn golden yellow.

Japanese pagodatrees typically grow to a height of 50 to 75 feet. Profuse clusters of creamy white, slightly fragrant flowers bloom in summer (this is one of the few trees with summer blooms).

Seedpods look somewhat like a pearl neck-lace—the pod is constricted between the seeds. They turn from green to yellow and finally yellowish brown and often remain on the tree into winter.

Yellowwood
Cladrastis kentukea

Leaves are alternate and range from 5 to 12 inches long. They have 5 to 11 unserrated leaflets, each 2 to 4 inches long, often arranged in an alternate manner on the main stem. The terminal leaflet is the largest; leaftlets at the base are smallest.

Leaves turn a deep yellow in autumn.

Yellowwood trees grow to 30 to 50 feet high.

White, fragrant flowers appear in late spring in large, drooping clusters.

Fruit is a 2- to 4-inch green or brownish pod (like a pea pod) with 4 to 6 flat, brown seeds inside.

Black Locust
Robinia pseudoacacia

Leaves are alternate, up to 14 inches long, and singly compound, with 7 to 19 oval, unserrated, 1-inch leaflets, each on a short stem.

Compare with honeylocust (page 58), whose leaflets have no stems, and European mountain-ash, whose leaflets are serrated.

Thorns or small spines may be present on the branches.

Black locust grows to a height of 80 feet.

White, fragrant flowers with yellow spots occur in mid to late spring in long (5 inches), drooping clusters.

Fruits are flat brown pods up to 6 inches long.

European Mountain-ash/Rowan
Sorbus aucuparia

Leaves are alternate and up to 8 inches long, with 9 to 19 oval, serrated leaflets—often with no teeth at the base.

Compare with black locust or honeylocust (page 58), whose leaves are not obviously serrated.

Leaves may be yellow, red, or reddish purple in autumn.

A small tree, European mountain-ash seldom grows more than 30 feet high.

Showy white flowers ($1/4$ inch) in clusters bloom in spring.

Colorful red berries appear (also in clusters) and mature in late summer.

Tree of Heaven/Ailanthus
Ailanthus altissima

Leaves are alternate, large (up to 24 inches long), and compound, with 11 to 41 leaflets.

The top leaflet may be toothed or lobed. The side leaflets are toothed only at the base of the leaflet, where there are 1 or 2 teeth on each side. Leaflets give off a foul odor when crushed.

Trees of heaven grow rapidly and can reach a height of 100 feet. The name comes from their height.

Seldom deliberately planted in parks or neighborhoods, the tree of heaven is often found along alleys, near railroads, or in unkempt parts of town.

Flowers are small and greenish, and grow in large clusters.

Seeds form in large clusters of dry, narrow-winged, twisted wafers—1 seed per wafer.

Staghorn Sumac
Rhus typhina

Leaves are alternate, up to 24 inches long, and compound, with 11 to 31 leaflets.

Leaflets are narrow, pointed, and serrated, and have no stems. The terminal leaflet may have 1 or 2 small lobes.

Staghorn sumacs are small trees or shrubs that reach a height of only 15 feet (occasionally taller). The tree is often found along the edge of woods along roadways.

Leaves turn bright red in early autumn, making this tree easy to recognize from a distance.

Flowers, tiny and green, appear in upright clusters in early summer. Male and female flowers grow on separate trees.

Fruits are red, dry, and hairy, and ripen in late summer. They form in dense, upright clusters, only on female trees.

Black Walnut
Juglans nigra

Leaves are alternate, grow up to 24 inches long, and have 15 to 23 leaflets. Crushed leaves have a spicy scent.

The leaflets are pointed and serrated, smooth on the top, and fuzzy underneath, and have no stems. They range from 2 to 5 inches in length; the ones near the middle of the stem are the longest. The terminal leaflet is often missing (as shown); if present, it is often smaller than those near it.

The leaves turn yellowish green in autumn.

Tiny green flowers grow in 2- to 4-inch-long clusters called catkins.

The fruit (nut) is black and forms in a round husk about 1 to 2 inches in diameter, green at first, then turning black. Nuts are found in pairs or small clusters.

Black walnut trees usually have tall trunks with no low branches and can grow to 50 to 75 feet high.

Goldenraintree
Koelreuteria paniculata

Leaves are alternate, 6 to 18 inches long, and bright green, with 7 to 15 coarsely serrated or slightly lobed leaflets. Occasionally the leaves are partially bipinnately compound. Leaves may turn yellowish in autumn.

Goldenraintree grows to a height of 30 to 40 feet.

Flowers bloom in mid summer. They are yellow, with 4 petals, about $1/2$ inch wide, in conical clusters about 15 inches high. Fruits grow in clusters at the ends of branches. Each one looks like a dry, three-sided balloon or capsule. They change in color from green to yellow and then brown. Seeds, found inside, are small, hard, and black.

Shagbark Hickory
Carya ovata

Leaves are alternate and 8 to 14 inches long, with 5 (sometimes 7) finely serrated, football-shaped leaflets, each 4 to 6 inches long.

Leaves are yellow-green in summer and turn yellow to golden brown in autumn.

Shagbark hickory grows to a height of 60 to 80 feet.

The bark on older trees breaks into hard plates that peel off at both ends, giving the tree a shaggy appearance.

The fruit is a nut in a 1- to $1^{1}/_{2}$-inch, brown (when ripe), 4-ribbed husk.

Shagbark hickory is the most common hickory in urban and suburban settings.

HICKORY TREES

Hickory leaves look somewhat like ash leaves but are alternate rather than opposite. Ash leaflets are also all about the same size, whereas hickory leaflets are largest at the top and progressively smaller down to the leaf base.

Male flowers (shown here) are catkins and obvious in mid spring. Female flowers are small and inconspicuous. The fruit is a nut enclosed in a 4-ribbed husk. Hickories have a taproot that makes them hard to transplant and thus have been less commonly planted in cities than many other species.

Bitternut Hickory
Carya cordiformis

Leaves are alternate and 6 to 10 inches long, with 7 (sometimes 5 or 9) serrated and narrow leaflets. Each leaflet is 3 to 6 inches long.

Leaves turn golden yellow in autumn.

The nuts are slightly smaller than shagbark's and very bitter (even squirrels are said to ignore them).

Bitternut hickory typically grows to a height of 50 to 75 feet.

Mockernut Hickory
Carya tomentosa

Leaves are alternate and 6 to 12 inches long, with 7 to 9 serrated and somewhat football-shaped leaflets. The backs of the leaflets are covered with tiny hairs or fuzz.

Leaves turn golden yellow in autumn.

The nuts are slightly larger (up to $1^3/4$ inches in diameter) than those of the other hickories.

The tree is easily distinguished from shagbark hickory because its bark is firm and tight.

Mockernut hickory typically grows to a height of 50 to 60 feet.

Green Ash
Fraxinus pennsylvanica

Leaves grow to 12 inches long. Leaflets are usually shiny and dark green on top, lighter and less shiny on the back.

Leaflets may have either smooth or finely and sharply serrated margins.

Most leaves turn yellow in autumn.

Leaf scars are semicircular with a flat or nearly flat top like a D on its side.

Green ash may grow to a height of 50 to 60 feet.

ASH TREES

Ash trees are relatively easy to identify as a group, but it requires careful observation to tell the different ash species apart. Green and white ash leaves are both oppositely attached and pinnately compound, with 5 to 13 (usually 7) oval leaflets—usually rounded at their bases and tapered to a point at the tips. Tiny male and female flowers, which grow on separate trees, have no petals. The female trees may have clusters of 1- to 2-inch tan samara (shaped like canoe paddles) that mature in autumn. Many cultivars are seedless, however.

White Ash

Fraxinus americana

Leaves grow to 15 inches long. Leaflets are usually dark green on top and whitish (or at least paler) on the back.

Leaflets may have either smooth or slightly wavy or scalloped margins.

Most leaves turn purple in autumn.

Leaf scar has a deep or shallow top notch, like a C on its side.

White ash may grow to a height of 60 to 80 feet.

Boxelder/Manitoba Maple/Ash Leaf Maple
Acer negundo

Leaves are opposite and compound, with 3 or 5 (sometimes 7 or 9) leaflets. They may be up to 12 inches long with a 2- to 3-inch leafstalk.

Leaflets have large teeth or shallow lobes and short stalks. They turn pale yellow in autumn.

Boxelder grows to a height of 30 to 50 feet. It is seldom planted in parks or residential neighborhoods.

Flowers are inconspicuous. Male and female flowers grow on separate trees.

Fruits (only on the females) are paired, winged seeds similar to those of other maples. They hang in clusters and ripen in autumn.

Paperbark Maple
Acer griseum

Leaves are opposite, compound, up to 6 inches long, and always with 3 toothed leaflets. The two side leaflets have no stems.

The leaves turn bronze in autumn.

Parperbark maple may grow to 20 to 30 feet high. Its distinctive, paper-thin bark is reddish brown and naturally peels off and curves backwards. Its flowers, when present, are green and inconspicuous.

The fruits are the typical maple pairs of winged seeds. The tree produces very few of them, however.

CHAPTER 5

Trees with Red or Purple Summer Leaves

Japanese Maple
Acer palmatum

Leaves are red or maroon, opposite, and small (2 to 4 inches), and have 5 to 9 narrow, serrated, palmate lobes. Leaves may also be green or "dissected" and look somewhat like lace.
See page 43 for full description.

Norway Maple
Acer platanoides

Leaves are maroon or dark purple and opposite, and have 5 to 7 palmate lobes with large, sharply pointed teeth and rounded sinuses between the lobes. They are up to 7 inches across and may also be green.
See page 44 for full description.

Eastern Redbud
Cercis canadensis

Heart-shaped leaves are maroon, alternate, smooth-edged, and up to 5 inches wide. Veins at the base of the leaf are palmate. Leaves may also be green.
See page 21 for full description.

Katsuratree
Cercidiphyllum japonicum

Leaves are red to maroon, opposite, 2 to $3^{1}/_{2}$ inches long, and somewhat heart shaped, and have blunt teeth. Veins at the base of the leaf are palmate. The leafstalk is $^{3}/_{4}$ to $1^{1}/_{2}$ inches long. Leaves may also be green.
See page 35 for full description.

Crabapple
Malus (species)

Leaves are alternate, roughly oval, up to 4 inches long, and serrated. Tip is pointed; the base may be heart shaped. Some leaves may have a couple of large teeth near the base. They may also be yellow-orange, green, or a mixture of red and green.
  See page 37 for full description.

Purple-leaf Plum
Prunus cerasifera 'Newport'

Bronze or purple leaves are alternate, oval, up to 2^1/$_2$ inches long and serrated, and may have pointed tips. Other varieties have green leaves.
  See page 38 for full description.

Purple Beech
Fagus sylvatica

Leaves are alternate, elliptical, smaller at up to 4 inches than American beech leaves (page 24), and more elliptical. Stems are longer than those of American beech.
  See page 24 for full description.

'Royal Purple' Smoketree
Cotinus coggygria 'Royal Purple'

Leaves are dark purple—almost black—alternate, oval, 1^1/$_2$ to 3^1/$_2$ inches long, and have smooth margins. Leaf stem is up to 1^1/$_2$ inches long.
  See page 19 for full description.

SPECIES INFORMATION

In this section, you will find information about the history, names, and uses of the trees found in this book, as well as the zones in which each is hardy. Zone numbers in parentheses mean that a species might be hardy in this zone if certain conditions (such as soil composition, altitude, or humidity) are favorable.

Ailanthus: *See* Tree of Heaven

Alder, Black; *Alnus glutinosa* (AL-nus glue-tih-NO-suh)

Alnus is the old Latin name for the alder tree. Native to Europe, North Africa, and western and northern Asia, it was introduced into North America during colonial times. Black alder is a fast-growing tree. The wood is soft, somewhat elastic, and easily worked; it's used for wooden carvings, cigar boxes, and shoes. The bark is used in tanning and gives a reddish color to leather. The leaves were used in a number of folk remedies for cancer and other illnesses.
Hardiness: Zones 4-7

Apple/Orchard Apple/Common Apple; *Malus x domestica* (MAY-lus doe-MESS-tih-kuh)

Malus is the ancient Latin name for the apple tree. The common apple is a hybrid native to Eurasia and was brought to North America before 1600. The trees were already growing wild on this continent long before Johnny Appleseed started taking them to pioneers in the Midwest. Most apple trees are grown for their fruit. Because the wood is hard, it is sometimes used for tool handles. The wood also makes good fuel and is occasionally used for smoking meats. The apple blossom is the state flower of Arkansas and Michigan. *See also* Crabapple.
Hardiness: Zones 4-7

Apple, Hedge: *See* Osage-Orange

Arborvitae/Northern White Cedar; *Thuja occidentalis* (THOO-yuh ock-sih-den-TAY-liss)

Arborvitae was the first tree introduced from Canada to Europe. Its common name comes from the Latin *arbor,* meaning "tree," and *vitae,* meaning "life," and refers to how French explorers in the 1530s used parts of the tree to cure scurvy. It is often used as an evergreen hedge. The wood is used commercially to make cedar shingles, shakes, and siding.
Hardiness: Zones 3-7

Ash, Green; *Fraxinus pennsylvanica* (FRAK-sih-nus pen-sil-VAN-ih-kuh)

Green ash is one of the most common trees in the urban forest, although once the emerald ash borer started infecting them, the trees disappeared from nurseries. Because its wood is strong yet somewhat elastic, green ash is used to make oars and canoe paddles.
Hardiness: Zones 2-9

Ash, White; *Fraxinus americana* (FRAK-sih-nus uh-mair-ih-CAN-uh)

White ash wood is lightweight, strong, and just slightly elastic, which makes it perfect for baseball bats. It's also used for hockey sticks, polo mallets, canoe paddles, boats, tool handles, and furniture, including church and railroad station pews. The name comes from the color of the wood.

Hardiness: Zones 4-9

Aspen, Bigtooth; *Populus grandidentata* (POP-yoo-lus gran-dih-den-TAH-tah)

Bigtooth aspen is one of the few trees whose name (both common and Latin) describes something about the shape of the leaf. The leaf's big, pointed teeth are an easy aid to identification. The wood is soft and used primarily for pulp. Other uses include making particleboard, log homes, boxes, ladders, chopsticks, and hockey stick components.

Hardiness: Zones 3-5 (6)

Aspen, Quaking; *Populus tremuloides* (POP-yoo-lus trem-you-LOY-deez)

Quaking aspen is found over a greater area than any other tree in North America (it's the only tree in this book hardy in zone 1). It is a cool-weather tree whose natural habitat ranges from mid-Canada to high altitudes as far south as central Mexico. It is one of the few trees whose name (both common and Latin) describes motion. Quaking aspen leaves flutter even in light breezes because their leafstalks are flattened parallel to the leaf surface, allowing them to easily bend back and forth. The wood is a major source of North American paper pulp; it's also used for barn floors, horse stalls, siding, fence posts, and excelsior (shavings used for packing).

Hardiness: Zones 1-6 (7)

Baldcypress; *Taxodium distichum* (tack-SO-dee-um DISS-tick-um)

The scientific name *taxodium* means "like *taxus*" (like the yew tree); *distichum* means "in two ranks". Both names refer to the needles. Baldcypress is native to the Southeast and is the state tree of Louisiana, but transplanted specimens grow quite well in northern areas. It is a deciduous conifer—it has needles, not broad leaves, and drops them every fall; it also drops the shoots on which the needles grow, giving the tree a "bald" appearance in winter. The tree was named Urban Tree of the Year for 2007 by the Society of Municipal Arborists in *City Trees* magazine because of its ease of maintenance, rapid growth, strong wood, and lack of serious problems with insects or disease.

Hardiness: Zones 4-10

Basswood, American/American Linden; *Tilia americana* (TILL-ee-uh uh-mair-ih-KAY-nuh)

According to the Ohio Department of Natural Resources, the American basswood is a favorite tree of honeybees, which make high-quality honey from its nectar. The tree's wood is weak, but because it's also lightweight and odorless, it's used for boxes and crates for food. The inner bark, however, is tough and has been used to make rope, mats, and bandages. The cultivar 'Redmond' was named Urban Tree of the Year in 2000.

Hardiness: Zones 3-8

Beech, American; *Fagus grandifolia* (FAY-gus gran-dih-FO-lee-uh)

The scientific name *grandifolia* means large leaf (even though the 6-inch leaves aren't all that large). American beech is a large, slow-growing shade tree. The wood is used for floors, furniture, appliance handles, toys, cutting boards, and beer barrels. Because it's resistant to decay underwater, it was once used to make waterwheels for gristmills. It was on an American beech tree in Tennessee that Daniel Boone made his famous inscription: "D. Boon Cilled A BAR On Tree In thE Year 1760." American beech is not as common in urban areas as the imported European beech.

Hardiness: Zones 4-9

Beech, Blue: *See* Hornbeam, American

Beech, European/Purple Beech/Tri-Color Beech; *Fagus sylvatica* 'Riversii'/'Tri-Color' (FAY-gus sill-VAT-ih-kuh)

The European beech, native to much of Europe, extending from Scandinavia south to central Spain and east to northwest Turkey, was brought to North American by the 1750s. The tree grows faster than its American cousin and has been somewhat more successful in urban sites. This species is the most variable of all ornamental shade trees. That, plus the intriguing, purple-leafed cultivars, has made it, even in North America, the more popular ornamental tree.

Hardiness: Zones 4-7

Birch, European White; *Betula pendula* (BET-oo-luh PEN-doo-luh)

The European white birch is native to much of Europe and western Asia and is the national tree of Finland. It was brought to Virginia during colonial times. Its popularity in North America is due largely to its unusual-shaped leaves and stunning white bark. It is often planted in groups of three. While most of these trees have green leaves, there are several cultivars with dark purple leaves. The tree is susceptible to several diseases as well as the bronze birch borer and so needs more care than many other ornamental trees. It is often short-lived. The Latin name *pendula* means hanging (as in pendant) and refers to the tree's drooping branches.

Hardiness: Zones 2-6 (7)

Birch, Paper/White Birch; *Betula papyrifera* (BET-oo-luh pap-i-RIF-er-uh)

Paper birch has a remarkable adaptability to heat and cold—surviving as far north as any North American trees. It is well known as the tree of choice for making birchbark canoes in days gone by. It got both its names from its very thin, paperlike bark, which peels off easily and was used for making notes and writing messages. The Latin *papyrifera* comes from the Egyptian word *papyrus,* meaning "paper." Paper birch is the state tree of New Hampshire and provincial tree of Saskatchewan.

Hardiness: Zones 2-6 (7)

Birch, Purple-leaf White

Purple-leaf cultivars of the European White Birch have dramatic, dark leaves, which has made them popular in residential areas despite their relative fragility.

Birch, River; *Betula nigra* (BET-oo-luh NYE-gruh)

Unlike other fast-growing trees, river birch is not brittle and is therefore seldom damaged by wind or ice. It is also highly resistant to the bronze birch borer. River birch is the only common city birch tree that releases its seeds in the spring. The cultivar 'Heritage' was named Urban Tree of the Year in 2002. It has great vigor and thrives in urban conditions; it is especially appreciated in the South because it is the only white-barked birch tree that can stand extreme heat. The wood is sometimes used for making cabinets or furniture.

Hardiness: Zones 3-9

Birch, White: *See* Birch, Paper

Blackgum: *See* Tupelo, Black

Boxelder/Manitoba Maple/Ash Leaf Maple; *Acer negundo* (AY-sir ne-GOON-doe)

The boxelder is seldom deliberately planted because the wood is weak and tends to break in high winds or ice storms. In addition, it is susceptible to trunk decay and the boxelder bug and is rather short lived. But it grows quickly and will thrive almost anywhere and so it can be desirable for some environments. It can be found in cities today in nonlandscaped locations. The name was given to it because it has been used for making crates, pallets, and boxes.

Hardiness: Zones 3-9

Buckeye, Ohio; *Aesculus glabra* (ES-kew-lus GLAY-bruh)

Not only is the Ohio buckeye the state tree of Ohio, "buckeye" is the state's nickname and name of The Ohio State University's athletic teams. Many folks in Ohio believe that holding a dry buckeye nut in the pocket brings good luck; some OSU fans make necklaces out of the dried nuts. The tree's lightweight wood is used to make artificial limbs.

Hardiness: Zones 4-7

Buckthorn, Common/European Buckthorn; *Rhamnus cathartica* (RAM-nus ka-THAR-ti-ka)

Buckthorn is a native of Eurasia and North Africa. It is a thorny, low-branched, adaptable plant, often surrounded by suckers at its base. It grows well in urban areas—so well that it soon can become a disliked weed.

Hardiness: Zones 3-7

Catalpa, Northern/Hardy Catalpa; *Catalpa speciosa* (Kuh-TAL-puh spee-see-O-suh)

Native from southern Indiana to northern Tennessee and Arkansas, catalpa is now widely planted as an ornamental. Its wood is not very flexible and so small branches often break in high winds. The wood near the ground, however, is very resistant to rot and has been used for fence posts and railroad ties.

Hardiness: Zones 4-8 (9)

Catalpa, Southern/Common Catalpa; *Catalpa bignonioides* (Kuh-TAL-puh BIG-known-e-OY-deez)

Catalpa is the Cherokee word for tree. *Bignonioides* refers to its trumpet-shaped flowers, which are similar to those of bignonia (the southern quartervine). Southern catalpa is native to the Southeast but is now grown as far north as southern Ontario. It's a popular shade tree but it's also planted because it's the host plant for the catawba worm caterpillar, a popular fish bait.

Hardiness: Zones 5-9

Cedar, Northern White: *See* Arborvitae

Cherry, Black; Prunus serotina (PROO-nus say-ROT-in-uh)

Black cherry wood is reddish brown, fine grained, and used for making furniture and high-quality veneers. The fragrant but bitter inner bark is used in wild cherry cough syrup.

Hardiness: Zones 3-9

Cherry, Weeping Higan; *Prunus subhirtella* 'Pendula' (PRU-nus sub-her-TEL-uh)

The weeping Higan cherry tree, an import from Japan, is a beautiful tree with branches that droop nearly to the ground—in spring, when the blossoms appear, it is downright spectacular.

Hardiness: Zones (4) 5-8

Cherry, Japanese Flowering; *Prunus serrulata*
(PRU-nus sair-yoo-LAY-tuh)

The Japanese flowering cherry cultivar 'Kwanzan' was among the 3,000 trees given to the United States by Japan in 1912. They were planted in Washington, DC, and now create spectacular displays each spring. The first annual Cherry Blossom Festival there was held in 1935. 'Kwanzan' is probably the hardiest Japanese flowering cherry cultivar today.

Hardiness: Zones 5-6 (some cultivars hardy farther south)

Coffeetree, Kentucky; *Gymnocladus dioicus*
(jim-NOK-la-dus dye-o-EE-kus)

Kentucky coffeetree was named Urban Tree of the Year in 2006 because of its adaptability to harsh urban conditions as well as its ornamental qualities. According to the Kentucky Department for Libraries and Archives, the tree got its name from early pioneers who brewed a coffeelike drink by putting its ground seeds in boiling water. The wood is sometimes called Kentucky mahogany because of its color and grain and has been used for making fence posts and furniture. The Latin name *gymnocladus* means "naked branch"; the tree's leaves emerge late in spring and drop early in fall. Kentucky coffeetree was the state tree of Kentucky from 1976 to 1994, when it was replaced by the tuliptree.

Hardiness: Zones 3-8

Cottonwood, Eastern; *Populus deltoides*
(POP-yoo-lus dell-TOY-deez)

You can almost identify cottonwood by its sound. Because its leafstalks are flat, the leaves flutter and seem to sing even in a slight breeze. The English name comes from the cottonlike fluff attached to its tiny seeds. The scientific name comes from the triangular Greek letter delta, and *oides,* meaning "resemblance," because the leaf is shaped somewhat like a triangle. Although they are great shade trees, cottonwoods are disliked by some because of those cottony seeds, which get blown by the wind every spring. As a result, cottonwood trees are seldom deliberately planted in cities; because they're fast growing, however, they are often planted in rural areas as windbreaks. Cottonwood bark, buds, and flowers have been used over the years in folk medicine. Today, the wood is used for lumber, veneers, excelsior, and fuel. It's the state tree of Kansas, Nebraska, and Wyoming.

Hardiness: Zones 3-9

Crabapple; *Malus (species)* (MAY-lus)

Crabapple trees are most noticeable in spring when they are in bloom. Unfortunately, most crabapple trees are susceptible to apple scab, leaf blot, rust, and powdery mildew that can leave a tree denuded of half its leaves by late summer. Still, this extremely popular tree is found in grassy areas near schools, libraries, and homes. Crabapple fruits, by definition, are smaller than 2 inches across. If it's larger, call it an apple.

Hardiness: Zones 4-8 (some cultivars may be hardy farther north or south)

Dogwood, Alternate Leaf/Pagaoda Dogwood; *Cornus alternifolia* (KOR -nus all-tur-nih-FO-lee-a)

This tree is native to eastern North America. It got one of its common names from its layers of horizontal branches that can look somewhat like a Japanese pagoda.

Hardiness: Zones 3-7

Dogwood, Flowering; *Cornus florida* (KOR-nus FLOR-ih-duh)

The flowering dogwood is the state tree of Missouri and Virginia; its blossom is the state flower of Virginia and North Carolina. Unfortunately, this tree is easily infected with anthracnose fungal disease. Historically, the hard, close-grained wood was used in the textile industry to make shuttles for weaving.

Hardiness: Zone 5-9a

Dogwood, Kousa; *Cornus kousa* (KOR-nus KOO-suh)

Kousa dogwood, native to eastern Asia, has become a popular small ornamental tree in North America because of its disease resistance, interesting shape, and long-lasting flowers. Its horizontal branches create a layered look that can soften the harsh, vertical lines of buildings.

Hardiness: Zones 5-8

Douglas-Fir; *Pseudotsuga menziesii* (SOO-doe-soo-gah men-ZEE-zee-eye)

Douglas-fir is native to the west coast of North America. It is one of our tallest trees, commonly growing to a height of more than 100 feet, sometimes upwards of 300 feet. Douglas-fir wood is strong, making it an important timber tree. Douglas-fir is not a true fir and not in the genus *Abies,* as is white fir. Its genus name means "false hemlock." Scottish naturalist Archibald Menzies found and described the tree in 1792. The name Douglas comes from David Douglas, who recognized the tree's value and sent seeds to Britain. Douglas-fir is the state tree of Oregon. The variety *glauca* is grown in the Midwest and Northeast and is a popular Christmas tree.

Hardiness: Zones (3) 4-6

Elm, American; *Ulmus americana* (UL-mus uh-mair-ih-KAY-nuh)

American elm trees are tall and have a regal, vaselike appearance. Although Dutch elm disease has killed nearly all American elm trees the areas it affects there are still thousands of these handsome trees gracing parks and residential streets. Fortunately, a few cultivars such as 'Valley Forge' and 'New Harmony' appear to be highly resistant (although not immune) to the disease—so the American elm may be making a comeback in our towns and cities. Elm wood is hard and difficult to split and so has been used for making hockey sticks as well as furniture, flooring, boxes, crates, barrels, and railroad ties; elm wood is used rarely commercially today, however.

Hardiness: Zones 3-9

Elm, Chinese/Lacebark Elm; *Ulmus parvifolia* (UL-mus par-vih-FO-lee-a)

Native to eastern Asia, the Chinese elm was brought to North America in 1794. Its scientific name comes from *parvus,* meaning "small," and *folia,* meaning "leaves." This elm tolerates urban conditions and is resistant to Dutch elm disease. The cultivar 'Allee' was named Urban Tree of the Year in 2003.

Hardiness: Zones (4) 5-9

Elm, Siberian; *Ulmus pumila* (UL-mus PEW-mih-luh)

Native to eastern Asia, the Siberian elm has a scientific name that means dwarf, although the trees planted in North America since 1905 have not been the small, shrublike variety for which the tree was named. Siberian elm was very popular in the 1930s—valued for its rapid growth, resistance to drought, and ability to grow in poor soil. Its wood is brittle, however. Its seeds, easily spread by the wind, have resulted in thousands of unwanted trees in pastures, along roads, and in alleys.

Hardiness: Zones 4-9

Elm, Slippery/Red Elm; *Ulmus rubra* (UL-mus ROO-bruh)

Slippery elm has sometimes been used as a landscape substitute for the American elm. It is not as large or as beautiful, however, and it is also susceptible to Dutch elm disease, so it has not become very popular. Its names come from the red color of its leaf buds in winter and the texture of its inner bark, which was once ground up and used as medicine.

Hardiness: Zones 3-9

Fir, White/Concolor Fir; *Abies concolor* (AY-beez KAWN-kull-er)

White fir wood is used for lumber, plywood, pulp, subflooring, siding, and paneling. The trees are also often used as Christmas trees because they have a dependable conical shape, good needle retention, and a pleasant aroma.

Hardiness: Zones 4-7

Ginkgo; *Ginkgo biloba* (GINK-go bye-LOE-buh)

The ginkgo tree is sometimes referred to as a living fossil because it is the only surviving species of a group of trees that were common in prehistoric times. A native of China, this tree was brought to North America by the 1780s. It is now widely planted in temperate regions worldwide because of its interesting shape and leaves, resistance to disease, and tolerance of air pollution. The scientific name *biloba* refers to the 2 lobes that are often seen on the leaves. In 1996, the ginkgo cultivar 'Princeton Sentry' was named Urban Tree of the Year.

Hardiness: Zones 4-8 (9)

Goldenraintree; *Koelreuteria paniculata* (Ko-leh-TAIR-ee-ah pen-ik-u-LA-tah)

Goldenraintree is a native of China and Korea was brought to North America in 1763. It is one of the few trees that have yellow flowers, and its common name refers to them. Its species name, *paniculata,* refers to its flowers, which appear in "panicles," large loose clusters (like lilac flowers). The tree is particularly liked because the large clusters of yellow summer flowers contrast so nicely with its green foliage. However, in late summer it may look unkempt when its seedpods turn brown. In China, this tree is planted on the graves of scholars. Goldenraintree was named the 2011 Urban Tree of the Year.

Hardiness: Zones 5-8

Hackberry; *Celtis occidentalis* (SEL-tis ox-i-den-TAL-iss)

Hackberry has been used as a substitute for American elm because its leaves are similar, as are its ascending branches, and it is not susceptible to Dutch elm disease. In pioneer days, the tree's tough and flexible wood was used for barrel hoops and flooring in cabins. The name comes from the Scottish tree hagberry.

Hardiness: Zones 3-9

Hawthorn, Cockspur; *Crataegus crusgalli* (kruh-TEE-gus kris-GALL-ee)

The thorns on this hawthorn can be up to 8 inches long. Their curved shape gave the tree both its scientific and English names; *crusgalli* means "the leg (or spur) of a rooster," or a cockspur. There are cultivars on the market that have no thorns.

Hardiness: Zones 4-6 (7)

Hawthorn, Downy/Red Hawthorn; *Crataegus mollis* (kruh-TEE-gus MOLL-lis)

Downy hawthorn is among the earliest of the hawthorns to bloom and have ripe fruit, which often remains on the tree when the leaves fall. Its leaves, somewhat fuzzy or hairy (thus its name) are larger than those of most other hawthorns.

Hardiness: Zones 3-6

Hawthorn, English/Midland Hawthorn; *Crataegus laevigata* (kruh-TEE-gus lee-vih-GAY-tuh)

This short, low-branching, ornamental tree was brought to North America by English colonists to be used in hedges, as it was used in England. It's sometimes called the midland hawthorn.

Hardiness: Zones 4-7

Hawthorn, Green/'Winter King' Hawthorn; *Crataegus viridis* (kruh-TEE-gus VEER-ih-diss)

'Winter King' is a popular cultivar of the green hawthorn. Horticulturalist Michael Dirr suggests that the tree is one of the "most outstanding hawthorns for landscape use." Its attractive, red fruits stay on the tree through the winter (unless the birds get them). Green hawthorn's scientific name *viridis,* not surprisingly, means "green."

Hardiness: Zones 4-7

Hawthorn, Washington; *Crataegus phaenopyrum* (kruh-TEE-gus fee-no-PYE-rum)

Many folks like the Washington hawthorn because its spring flowers bloom after all the other hawthorns' blooms have faded. A major drawback is the presence of thorns, which gave the tree its name. The cultivar 'Princeton Sentry' is almost thornless.

Hardiness: Zones 4-8

Hedge Apple: *See* Osage-Orange

Hemlock, Eastern/Canadian Hemlock; *Tsuga canadensis* (TSOO-guh kan-uh-DEN-sis)

Very shade tolerant and graceful, eastern hemlock is easy to trim and shape and is thus often used as a foundation planting around houses or commercial buildings. The wood is brittle and splits easily and thus has little use as lumber. Eastern hemlock is the state tree of Pennsylvania. Western hemlock, *Tsuga heterophylla,* is the state tree of Washington.

Hardiness: Zones 3-7 (8)

Hickory, Bitternut; *Carya cordiformis* (KAY-ree-uh cord-ih-FOR-miss)

The fastest growing of the hickory trees, the bitternut may be best known for the use of its wood in smoking meats. Years ago, North American pioneers are said to have extracted the oil from its nuts for use in lamps.

Hardiness: Zones 4-9

Hickory, Mockernut; *Carya tomentosa* (KAY-ree-uh toe-men-TOE-suh)

The scientific name *tomentosa* means "woolly, with soft, matted hair," which refers to the soft fuzz on the backs of the tree's leaves. The wood is hard, resilient, and often used to make tool handles.
Hardiness: Zones 4-9

Hickory, Shagbark; *Carya ovata* (KAY-ree-uh oh-VAH-tuh)

Not surprising, this tree has shaggy, ragged-looking bark, which makes the tree easy to identify and probably is responsible for its being the most common hickory in cities and towns today. The species name *ovata* means "egg" and refers to the shape of the nut husks. In past days, the wood was used to make wheels for wagons and carriages as well as Native American bows. Today, the wood is used for furniture, flooring, tool handles, ladder rungs, and gymnasium equipment, while pieces of the bark are used to provide a hickory flavor when barbequing.
Hardiness: Zones 4-8

Holly, American; *Ilex opaca* (EYE-lex oh-PAY-kuh)

The American holly, the state tree of Delaware, has about the whitest wood of all North American trees. Hard but not strong, it is used for cabinet inlays, brush handles, small pieces of furniture, and measuring scales and rules for scientific instruments. The wood can be dyed black to resemble ebony and used for piano keys and violin pegs. The leaves are best known for their use in Christmas decorations.
Hardiness: Zones 5-9

Holly, English/Meserve Hybrid Holly; *Ilex aquifolium/x meserveae* (EYE-lex a-kwi-FOL-ee-um, ex mez-ERV-ee-ay)

Hybrid hollies developed in the 1950s by Kathleen Meserve, who crossed the English holly with the prostrate holly, are very popular in the United States. Cultivars include 'Blue Prince,' 'Blue Princess,' 'Berri-Magic,' and 'Royal Family.' These hybrids are popular foundation plants because they can be trimmed so easily. Left alone, several cultivars may grow as high as 12 to 15 feet.
Hardiness: Zones 3-7

Honeylocust; *Gleditsia triacanthos*
(gleh-DIT-see-uh try-uh-KAN-thoas)

A popular lawn tree because its growth habit and small leaflets let light filter through, allowing grass to grow right up to its trunk. Honeylocust is unique in the city in that it often has both pinnately and bipinnately compound leaves on the same tree. The name "honey" came from the honeylike liquid found in its seedpods. Cultivars today are nearly fruitless and do not have the long thorns that were common on the original species. The cultivar 'Skyline' was named Urban Tree of the Year in 1999; it is nearly thornless and fruitless, has more upright branches, and is more cold-hardy than other varieties of the tree.
Hardiness: Zones 4-9

Hophornbeam, Eastern/Eastern Hornbeam/Ironwood;
Ostrya virginiana (OSS-tree-uh ver-jin-ee-AY-nuh)

The "hop" part of this tree's name comes from its fruits, which resemble hops that are used to make beer. "Hornbeam" refers to a similar tree in Europe whose wood was used to yoke oxen (a "beam" used to yoke "horned" beasts of burden). Tree expert Lee Jacobson describes the hophornbeam as an unglamorous but trouble-free tree that offers "subtle beauty of form and foliage."
Hardiness: Zones 3-9

Hornbeam, American/Blue Beech/Ironwood; *Carpinus caroliniana*
(kar-PYE-nus kair-oh-lin-ee-AY-nuh)

American hornbeam is a handsome landscape tree but not well known and often confused with both the hophornbeam and beech trees. Fortunately, its distinctive seeds, with their 3 green, leafy bracts, can be found on the tree much of the summer and fall. Its bark may be gray and smooth, giving the appearance of muscles and providing the tree with the nicknames "musclewood," and "ironwood."
Hardiness: Zones 3-9

Horsechestnut, Common; *Aesculus hippocastanum*
(ESS-kew-lus hip-oh-kass-TAY-num)

The horsechestnut is native to southeastern Europe. It is most striking in the spring, when its large clusters of showy flowers are in bloom. The tree tolerates urban conditions especially well. Both the English and scientific names come from the similar appearance of the horsechestnut seed to the edible seeds of the American chestnut tree. *Hippo* means "horse," and *kastanon* means "chestnut." A medicine for treating coughs in horses was once made from its seeds.
Hardiness: Zones 4-7

Horsechestnut, Red; *Aesculus x carnea*
(ESS-kew-lus ex KAR-nee-uh)
Red horsechestnut is a hybrid of *Aesculus hippocastanum* developed about 1812 in Europe. It's been available in North America since 1850 and is today probably the most common large, red-flowering tree in temperate cities and towns. Its scientific name *carnea* is from the Latin word for meat and refers to the flowers' red coloring.

Hardiness: Zones 4-7

Ironwood: *See* Hophornbeam, Eastern, *or* Hornbeam, American

Juneberry: *See* Serviceberry, Downy

Juniper, Eastern: *See* Redcedar, Eastern

Katsuratree; *Cercidiphyllum japonicum*
(ser-sih-dih-FILL-um juh-PAWN-ih-kum)
From its fossils, we know that the katsuratree once grew across much of North America and Europe. It disappeared from these areas during the Ice Age, surviving only in eastern Asia. It was then reintroduced in North America around 1865.

Hardiness: Zones 4-8

Lilac, Japanese Tree; *Syringa reticulata*
(sih-RING-guh reh-tick-yoo-LAY-tuh)
The Japanese tree lilac is in the same genus as the popular lilac bushes that are found in yards throughout temperate America; it is the only member of that group, however, that has the size and shape of a tree. It is native to northern Japan and was introduced into the United States in 1876 at Boston's Arnold Arboretum. The scientific name *syrinx* means "pipe" and refers to the tree's hollow stems. In 1997, the cultivar 'Ivory Silk' was named Urban Tree of the Year partly because of its success growing in areas affected by air pollution, poor drainage, compacted soil, and drought.

Hardiness: Zones 3-7

Linden, American: *See* Basswood, American

Linden, Littleleaf; *Tilia cordata* (TILL-ee-uh kor-DAY-tuh)
Horticulturalist Michael Dirr calls this native of Europe and the Caucasus Mountains an "excellent shade tree for lawn, large areas, streets . . . about any place a real quality tree is desired." It has dozens of cultivars.

Hardiness: Zones 3-7

**Locust, Black; *Robinia pseudoacacia*
(ro-BIN-ne-uh soo-doe-uh-KAY-sha)**
Because they resist rotting, black locust logs make fine railroad ties, fence posts, and telephone poles. The tree is susceptible to pests, such as the locust borer, however, which can easily destroy it. It is not recommended for landscaping and is found today primarily in nonlandscaped areas.
Hardiness: Zones 4-8

**Magnolia, Saucer; *Magnolia soulangeana*
(mag-NO-lee-uh soo-lan-jee-AY-nuh)**
Whereas the parents of the saucer magnolia are native to east Asia, this hybrid was developed in France. Saucer magnolias were brought to North America around 1830. The Chinese name for these magnolias, which means "welcoming spring flower," is appropriate because they are often the first to bloom in spring. Horticulturalist Michael Dirr notes that the tree is "overused but with ample justification." A similar magnolia tree *(Magnolia grandiflora)* is the state tree of Mississippi, and its blossom is the state flower of Mississippi and Louisiana.
Hardiness: Zones 4-9

Magnolia, Star; *Magnolia stellata* (mag-NO-lee-uh stell-AY-tuh)
The star magnolia, a native of Japan, was brought to North America in 1862. Its popularity is due to its abundance of white, starlike flowers with 9 to 20 long, narrow tepals (petals); the flowers appear before the leaves do. A shrub or small tree, it may bloom before it reaches 2 feet tall.
Hardiness: Zones 4-8 (9)

Maple, Amur; *Acer ginnala* (AY-sir jin-NAY-luh)
The Amur maple is a small tree native to Japan and northern China. It was introduced into the United States around 1860. This tree is useful for patios or against the walls of buildings to soften their appearance.
Hardiness: Zones 3-8

Maple, Ash Leaf: *See* Boxelder

**Maple, Bigleaf/Oregon Maple; *Acer macrophyllum*
(AY-sir MAC-roe-PHIL-um)**
Both the English and scientific names refer to its large leaves (*macro* means "large," *phylum* means "leaf"), the largest in the maple family. Its wood has been used to make furniture; its sap, like the sugar maple's, can be tapped to make syrup.
Hardiness: Zones 3-9

Maple, Freeman/'Autumn Blaze' Maple; *Acer x freemanii* 'Jeffersred' (AY-ser ex free-MAH-nee)

This cultivar was developed by nurseryman Glenn Jeffers in the late 1960s. It has been available for sale since about 1980 and has become very popular. Like the silver maple, it grows quickly (about four times faster than red maple). Unlike the silver maple, it is not terribly susceptible to storm damage. In autumn, its leaves turn a brilliant orange-red. It was named Urban Tree of the Year in 2004.

Hardiness: Zones 3-8

Maple, Hedge; *Acer campestre* (AY-ser kam-PES-tree)

As can be assumed from its name, hedge maple can be pruned and grown as a hedge. It is often found this way in Europe, where it is native. It is adaptable, grows well in well-drained soils, and is tolerant of drought.

Hardiness: Zones (4) 5-8

Maple, Japanese; *Acer palmatum* (AY-ser pal-MAY-tum)

The Japanese maple is a popular ornamental tree because of its compact size, leaf colors, and shape. The red-leaf cultivars are the most popular. It is sometimes found with a single trunk like the larger maples, sometimes like a shrub with multiple stems.

Hardiness: Zones 5-8 (some cultivars do less well in zone 5)

Maple, Manitoba: *See* Boxelder

Maple, Norway; *Acer platanoides* (AY-ser plat-uh-NOY-deez)

Norway maple is a dense shade tree imported from Europe by at least 1750, when it was noted to be in Philadelphia. It is now the second most common street tree in the Midwest. The name *platanoides* means "like the planetree" (sycamore or London planetree) with which it is often confused. Norway maple has a large number of popular cultivars, including 'Schwedleri,' whose leaves change color from maroon in spring to bronze-green in summer, and 'Crimson King,' whose leaves keep their maroon color from spring to fall. In Europe, Norway maple is an important timber tree because its wood is hard; it often grows there to 100 feet high.

Hardiness: Zones 4-7

Maple, Paperbark; *Acer griseum* (AY-ser GRIS-ee-um)

Paperbark maple is a favorite landscape plant because of its interesting, thin, cinnamon-colored bark that splits and peels back, exposing its underside. The tree is a native of west China and was imported into North America in 1907. Unfortunately, it is not common because it produces few seeds (a bonus to those who own them).

Hardiness: Zones 3-7 (8)

Maple, Red/Swamp Maple; *Acer rubrum* (AY-ser ROO-brum)

According to the Arbor Day Foundation, the red maple, which can be found from Newfoundland to Florida, has the greatest north-south range of any tree in the eastern forests. Red maple is one the earliest of the maples to bloom. When it is in bloom, the abundant but very tiny flowers give the tree a reddish blush, making it easy to identify from a distance. Red maple is a favorite in the city largely because of its brilliant red color in autumn. It is the state tree of Rhode Island.

Hardiness: Zones 3-9

Maple, Silver; *Acer saccharinum* (AY-ser sack-uh-RYE-num)

Its fast, dependable growth has made silver maple a relatively inexpensive tree, and thus it has been widely planted in cities and towns. Its heavy seed-fall in the spring, easily broken limbs, and dull autumn color have made it less desirable than other available street trees, however. Silver maple sap is superior (for making maple syrup) to that of other maple trees, according to many, but the sap flow is too slow for the tree to be used for commercial production.

Hardiness: Zones 3-9

Maple, Sugar; *Acer saccharum* (AY-ser sack-AR-rum)

Sugar maple trees have been highly valued for centuries. Native Americans knew them well and used their hardened sap as money. Maple sugar, maple syrup, and maple candy all are made from the sap of the sugar maple tree today. The wood has a beautiful grain and is extremely hard and so has been used for all kinds of goods, from fine furniture to bowling pins, baseball bats, and high-quality cutting blocks. The sugar maple leaf is the emblem of Canada and the tree is the state tree of New York, Vermont, West Virginia, and Wisconsin.

Hardiness: Zones 3-8

Mountain-ash, European/Rowan; *Sorbus aucuparia* (SOR-bus aw-kew-PAIR-ee-uh)

Native to Europe and Asia, the European mountain ash has been planted in North America since colonial days. Its English name comes from the fact that this tree grows at a higher altitude in the highlands of Scotland than any other tree. The alternate name Rowan comes from the Old English *raun,* meaning "red"—referring to its red berries or perhaps its fall coloring. The wood is sometimes used for lumber and tool handles.

Hardiness: Zones 3-6

Mulberry, Red; *Morus rubra* (MOE-russ ROO-bruh)

Red mulberry, an American native, is much less common in cities and towns than is the imported white mulberry. It is usually found in moist, shady, and naturally wooded locations.

Hardiness: Zones 5-9

Mulberry, White; *Morus alba* (MOE-russ AL-buh)

The white mulberry is a native of China, where it has been cultivated for more than 4,800 years for the silk industry. It was introduced into North America through Mexico in 1522 and then into Jamestown, Virginia, during colonial times. The tree was widely planted until people realized that silk production was too costly an endeavor. Now the tree is widespread throughout the warm and temperate parts of the continent—usually along railroad tracks, back alleys, and other nonlandscaped areas. Today, white mulberry trees are considered nuisance trees because their fruits, often eaten by birds and released in their feces, distribute thousands of seeds and stain sidewalks and laundry left outside to dry. The wood is durable although fairly soft and is used for furniture and shipbuilding.

Hardiness: Zones (4) 5-8 (9)

Oak, Black; *Quercus velutina* (KWER-kus vel-OO-teen-uh)

Black oaks are seldom seen in landscaped areas. In towns and cities, they are usually found in parks composed of natural landscapes (with trees that were there before the park was built). The wood is not commercially important.

Hardiness: Zones 3-9

Oak, Bur; *Quercus macrocarpa* (KWER-kus mack-roe-KAR-puh)

A bur oak was a welcome sight in pioneer days because its strong wood could be used to replace wagon wheels or tongues. Today, the bur oak is taking its place as a great urban tree. In 2001, it was named Urban Tree of the Year.

Hardiness: Zones 3-8

Oak, Chinkapin; *Quercus muehlenbergii* (KWER-kus mew-len-BER-jee-eye)

Chinkapin oak may not be as well known as red, black, or white oak, but it surely was known to the pioneers of Ohio, Indiana, and Kentucky, who used thousands of linear feet of this wood to make fences. The wood was also used for railroad ties for all the new railroads that began crossing the Midwest. Today, the Chinkapin oak is valued as an ornamental tree in parks and along city streets. In 2009, it was named Urban Tree of the Year.

Hardiness: Zones 4-7

Oak, English/Pedunculate Oak; *Quercus robur* (KWER-kus ROE-ber)

A massive tree (75 to 100 feet tall in North America, up to 150 feet in England) with extremely hard wood, English oak has been used for over 2,000 years. According to horticulturalist Arthur Lee Jacobson, this is the oak of the ancient Druids, of King Arthur's round table, Robin Hood's cudgel, and yule logs. The tree is native to Europe and North Africa and has been cultivated in North America since colonial times.

Hardiness: Zones 4-8

Oak, Pin; *Quercus palustris* (KWER-kus pal-US-triss)

Pin oak is one of the fastest-growing oaks. Unlike the black and white oak trees, the pin oak has a fibrous rather than long taproot. Thus, the tree is easy to transplant. These features have made pin oak the most common oak tree in towns and cities of temperate North America.

Hardiness: Zones 4-8

Oak, Red/Northern Red Oak; *Quercus rubra* (KWER-kus ROO-bruh)

Red oak is the tallest oak (over 100 feet) in the wild. In cities, it still grows to a stately 60 to 75 feet. Red oaks often are 25 to 50 years old before they begin to flower and grow acorns. A bit less common on the street than pin oak, red oak also grows rapidly (for an oak) and is easy to transplant. It is the state tree of New Jersey and provincial tree of Prince Edward Island.

Hardiness: Zones 3-7 (8)

Oak, Shingle/Laurel Oak; *Quercus imbricaria* (KWER-kus im-brih-KAIR-ee-uh)

Although shingle oak transplants easily, it isn't one of the more glamorous oaks and, perhaps because it doesn't have the familiar oak leaf lobes, isn't very popular. Shingle oak's common name comes from the story that early pioneers, at least in Illinois, are said to have used its narrowly split wood to produce shingles for their cabins, probably for want of a better species.

Hardiness: Zones 4-8

Oak, Swamp White; *Quercus bicolor* (KWER-kus BYE-kull-er)

Unlike the better-known white oak, swamp white oak does not have a long taproot and is therefore easier to transplant. It was named Urban Tree of the Year in 1998. The wood is not used much commercially because it is rather knotty.

Hardiness: Zones 4-8

Oak, White; *Quercus alba* (KWER-kus AL-buh)

White oak is a strong, sturdy tree and the state tree of Connecticut, Maryland, and Illinois. Its wood is well known for its use in furniture, kitchen cabinets, and hardwood flooring.

Hardiness: Zones 3-9

Olive, Russian; *Elaeagnus angustifolia* (eel-ee-AG-nus an-gus-tih-FO-lee-uh)

Native to southern Europe and western and central Asia, Russian olive was introduced into North America in the late 1800s. It is tolerant of sun, drought, poor soils, and salt. Its branches are sometimes thorny.

Hardiness: Zones 2-7

Osage-Orange/Hedge-apple; *Maclura pomifera* (Ma-KLUR-uh poe-MIFF-ur-uh)

The name comes from the Osage Indians of the Great Plains and the similarity of the tree's fruits to oranges. The trees are used for hedges in the plains states, where their durability is a real asset. The wood, tough and rot resistant, is used for fence posts, furniture, and bows.

Hardiness: Zones 4-9

Pagodatree, Japanese/Chinese Scholar-tree; *Sophora japonica* (So-FOR-uh juh-PON-ik-uh)

Native to East Asia, this tree was introduced into North America around 1811. In China, its name means "tree of success in life." It is liked particularly because of its showy display of flowers in summer. A good urban tree, it withstands drought, air pollution, and heat.

Hardiness: Zones 4-7

Pawpaw; *Asimina triloba* (uh-SIM-in-nuh try-LOE-buh)

Sometimes called the Indiana banana, the pawpaw is the only member of a family of tropical plants that grows in Canada and the northern U.S. Its twigs are a source of chemicals that are used for anticancer drugs and pesticides.

Hardiness: Zones 5-8

Peach; *Prunus persica* (PROO-nus PER-sick-uh)

Peaches were grown in China more than 3,000 years ago. Peach trees were introduced into Persia (now Iran) around the second century BCE; the Romans found them there and took them to Italy. They were among the first plants introduced into colonial America; records show that they were in Virginia as early as 1633. The Latin name *persica* was given to the tree because the namers wrongly believed that the tree originated in Persia. The peach blossom is the state flower of Delaware.

Hardiness: Zones 5-9

Pear, Callery; *Pyrus calleryana* (PIE-rus kal-ler-ee-AY-nuh)

Callery pear is a native of China. In 1918, seeds were brought to the United States as a possible rootstock for commercial pear trees. One of the trees grown from this seed, named 'Bradford,' was found to be exceptionally beautiful, with attractive spring flowers. The tree was cultivated and, beginning in the early 1960s, widely sold as an ornamental. Unfortunately, it was later found to have poorly attached limbs, and the trees suffered much damage during storms. Today, stronger cultivars such as 'Chanticleer' and 'Aristocrat' have replaced 'Bradford' at landscape centers. In 2005, 'Chanticleer' was named Urban Tree of the Year.

Hardiness: Zones 5-8 (9)

**Persimmon, Common; *Diospyros virginiana*
(dye-OSS-pih-ross ver-jin-nee-AY-nuh)**
Persimmon trees grow well in urban and suburban areas—they are not much affected by air pollution, compacted soil, drought, or poor drainage. The scientific name comes from *dios,* meaning "divine," and *pyros,* meaning "grain," so *diospyros* means "heavenly food." Persimmon wood is very fine grained, and because it doesn't crack, it was once used for golf club heads and billiard sticks.
     Hardiness: Zones 4-9

Pine, Black/Austrian Pine; *Pinus nigra* (PIE-nus NYE-gruh)
The black pine is a native of Austria and southern Europe. It was brought to North America in 1759. This evergreen tree is popular because of its dark green needles, attractive form, and tolerance of salt spray and air pollution. It also transplants easily and so is more common in urban areas than the similar-looking native red pine. Because of its adaptability, more than 217 million black pines were planted, beginning in 1935, in the dust bowl Shelterbelt Project.
     Hardiness: Zones 4-7

Pine, Eastern White; *Pinus strobus* (PIE-nus STROE-bus)
Eastern white pine is the tallest tree in the forests of eastern North America. It is the state tree of Maine and Michigan and the provincial tree of Ontario. White pine is a favorite evergreen tree for lawns and parks largely because of its soft, fragrant, and featherlike needles. It is also a very valuable timber tree, providing lumber that doesn't easily warp and is easy for carpenters to work. A "soft" pine, it is North America's most common softwood lumber, used for general construction work as well as doors, paneling, plywood, moldings, furniture, and cabinets. It is easily stained to almost any color. The white pine "cone and tassel" (a tassel is a cluster of 5 pine needles) is the state "flower" of Maine, known as the Pine Tree State.
     Hardiness: Zones 3-7 (8)

Pine, Jack; *Pinus banksiana* (PIE-nus bank-see-AY-nah)
Jack pine is a very cold-tolerant pine tree that can grow in poor, sandy soils. It is a pioneer tree, often the species that starts growing first after a forest fire. The lumber is used for pulp. Jack pine doesn't have much ornamental value. Its sometimes scruffy appearance gives it the nickname scrub pine. The Latin name comes from botanist Joseph Banks (1743-1820).
     Hardiness: Zones 2-6 (7)

Pine, Loblolly; *Pinus taeda* (PIE-nus TEE-da)

Loblolly pine is a fast-growing tree, easily transplanted and adaptable to different growing conditions. It doesn't do well in cold areas but is common in the South. It is the most important commercial tree there, sold as "southern yellow pine" and used for plywood, pulp, and paper. Its sap (pitch) is used to make turpentine and rosin for violin bows. Loblolly pine is the state tree of Arkansas.

Hardiness: Zones 6-9

Pine, Ponderosa; *Pinus ponderosa* (PIE-nus pon-dur-O-sah)

Ponderosa pine is native to western North America, where it is widely grown. It is not only a great landscape tree, it is also the source of more lumber than any other American pine tree—used for paneling, cabinets, doors, and trim. The name comes from the Latin word for ponderous or heavy, which well describes its hard wood. Ponderosa pine is the state tree of Montana.

Hardiness: Zones 3-6 (7)

Pine, Red; *Pinus resinosa* (PIE-nus rez-in-OH-suh)

Red pine is the state tree of Minnesota. It reaches its best development in the Upper Great Lakes, where it can grow to a trunk diameter of 2 to 4 feet. It is used in building construction and shipbuilding and as a pulpwood. It is less suited to urban areas than are the other pine trees listed here.

Hardiness: Zones 2-5

Pine, Scots/Scotch Pine; *Pinus sylvestris* (PIE-nus sil-VES-tris)

Scots pine is the most widespread pine tree on earth—growing today from the Atlantic to the Pacific in Eurasia, where it is native, and in North America, where it was introduced in the 1750s. In Europe, Scots pines are important timber trees, harvested when fully grown. In North America, trees grown commercially are cut down when young and sold as Christmas trees.

Hardiness: Zones 3-7

Pine, Western White; *Pinus monticola* (PIE-nus mon-tic-O-la)

Western white pine is similar to the more widespread eastern white pine but, as the name suggests, is found in the western parts of North America. Western white pine is the state tree of Idaho. It has soft, beautiful wood and is used to make paneling, doors, and trim. It is also the tree of choice for matchsticks.

Hardiness: Zones 5-7 (8)

Planetree, American: *See* Sycamore, American

Planetree, London; *Platanus x acerifolia* (PLAT-uh-nus ex ass-er-ih-FO-lee-uh)

The London planetree is a hybrid of the Asian and American planetrees. It was developed in England, perhaps as early as 1645. The tree is tolerant of smoke and air pollution and more resistant to the anthracnose fungus. It has become a common boulevard tree in Britain, Europe, and North America. The planetree is the tallest tree species in London and New York City. It may be the city's most interesting-looking tree in the winter. The name *acerifolia* means "maple leaf," which London planetree leaves resemble.

Hardiness: Zones (4) 5-8 (9)

Plum, Purple Leaf; *Prunus cerasifera* (PROO-nus sair-uh-SIFF-er-uh)

The purple leaf plum is one of several cultivars of the cherry plum tree, native to Eurasia. The cultivar 'Newport,' developed by the University of Minnesota in 1913, is named after a town in that state, and (not surprisingly) is one of the most successful cultivars in the north.

Hardiness: Zones (4) 5-8

Poplar, White; *Populus alba* (POP-yoo-lus AL-buh)

White poplar is sought after because of its unusual leaves. The cultivar 'Pendula' has a weeping form. 'Bolleana,' probably the most popular cultivar, is tall and narrow and has irregularly lobed leaves. White poplar is a native of Eurasia, introduced into North America in 1748 as an ornamental. Its success in here has meant that it has spread from urban areas into forests, where it is, unfortunately, replacing native trees.

Hardiness: Zones 3-8 (9)

Poplar, Yellow: *See* Tuliptree

Redbud, Eastern; *Cercis canadensis* (SER-sis kan-uh-DEN-sis)

The flowering of the redbud is a sure sign that spring has arrived. Redbud flowers have long been a welcome sight in natural areas as well as in city yards and parks. George Washington's diary notes his appreciation of the beauty of the tree and how he spent many hours transplanting seedlings from a nearby forest. Redbud is the state tree of Oklahoma and was named the 2010 Urban Tree of the Year.

Hardiness: Zones 4-9

**Redcedar, Eastern/Eastern Juniper; *Juniperus virginiana*
(joo-NIP-er-us ver-jin-ee-AY-nuh)**
Eastern redcedar is a slow-growing, ornamental evergreen tree with wood that's probably best known as a moth repellant in cedar chests and closets. It's also used for fence posts, furniture, and souvenirs and was once used for pencils. The tree is also sold as a Christmas tree. Eastern redcedar is one of the longest-living trees included here: The oldest on record is a Missouri tree more than 800 years old. The popular and commercial name redcedar is disliked by many botanists because the tree is actually a juniper, not a true cedar.
Hardiness: Zones 3-9

Rose of Sharon; *Hibiscus syriacus* (high-BISS-kuss seer-ee-AY-kuss)
The Latin name for the Rose of Sharon was given to it because it was believed at the time to have come from Syria. In fact, the tree is a native of India and China. It is widely planted today because it is one of the few trees that bloom profusely in late summer.
Hardiness: Zones 5-9

Rowan: *See* Mountain-ash, European

Sassafras; *Sassafras albidum* (SASS-uh-frass AL-bih-dum)
Sassafras is a favorite tree because of its three different leaf shapes and brilliant fall color. Unfortunately, it is not easy to transplant because of its long taproot and so is not very common in landscaped urban areas. More often, it is found in natural or wooded parklands. Oils, used in perfumed soaps, can be obtained from the roots and bark of sassafras trees. A delicious sassafras iced tea is made by boiling the bark of the roots and then pouring the liquid over ice.
Hardiness: Zones 4-9

Scholar-tree, Chinese: *See* Pagodatree, Japanese

**Serviceberry, Downy/Juneberry/Shadbush; *Amelanchier arborea*
(am-meh-LANG-kee-er ar-BORE-ee-uh)**
Serviceberry is a native of Eastern North America. It and other serviceberries (Allegheny serviceberry, *Amelanchier laevis,* and the hybrid *Amelanchier x grandiflora*) are all small trees that have spectacular fall color.
Hardiness: Zones 4-9

Shadbush: *See* Serviceberry, Downy

**Smoketree, Common/'Royal Purple' Smoketree; *Cotinus coggygria*
(koe-TYE-nus koe-GUY-gree-uh)**
Native to Eurasia, the smoketree was brought to North America by the 1790s. The plant grows naturally like a shrub but can be pruned to give it a treelike appearance. Its popularity comes from the spent flower stalks, which give the tree a smoky appearance in summer.
Hardiness: Zones (4) 5-8

Spruce, Colorado/Colorado Blue Spruce; *Picea pungens* (PIE-see-uh PUN-jenz)

Colorado spruce, native to the Rocky Mountains, has either green or bluish needles. The blue cultivars are very popular, and it is rare now to not see at least one blue spruce in a residential neighborhood. The scientific name *pungens* means "piercing," referring to the sharpness of the needles. Colorado spruce is the state tree of Utah and, naturally, Colorado.

Hardiness: Zones 3-7 (8)

Spruce, Norway; *Picea abies* (PIE-see-uh AY-beez)

Native to northern and central Europe and Asia, Norway spruce is a major timber tree in Europe. The wood is also used to make sounding boards for musical instruments. It's a popular ornamental evergreen in North America because of its deep green color, relatively fast growth rate, and characteristic drooping secondary branches.

Hardiness: Zones 3-7 (8)

Spruce, White; *Picea glauca* (PIE-see-uh GLAW-kuh)

The state tree of South Dakota and provincial tree of Manitoba, white spruce is a long-lived tree that is a valuable source of construction lumber and pulp. It is the most cold-hardy spruce, seldom found in the South.

Hardiness: Zones 2-6

Sumac, Staghorn; *Rhus typhina* (roose ty-FEE-nuh)

Staghorn sumac trees are not often found in landscaped areas. They're mostly along highways or somewhat wild natural areas in towns. The wood is soft and brittle, used commercially only for small items such as napkin rings.

Hardiness: Zones 4-8

Sweetgum; *Liquidambar styraciflua* (lick-wid-AM-bar sty-rass-ih-FLOO-uh)

Native to the Southeast, the sweetgum tree doesn't fare well in the far north. Sweetgum is a favorite ornamental tree because of its striking, star-shaped leaves. The fruits, which look like spiky gumballs, can be a nuisance, but since they remain on the tree through winter, they make winter identification easy. The earliest known record of the tree appears in a 1651 Spanish report in which it is noted that the tree produces a fragrant gum resembling liquid amber (the scientific name comes from this feature). Sweetgum wood is sometimes used for furniture and interior wood trim.

Hardiness: Zones 5-9

Sycamore, American/American Planetree; *Platanus occidentalis* (PLAT-uh-nus ock-sih-den-TAY-liss)

The largest (but not tallest) of all American broad-leafed trees, the American sycamore is more at home in the forest than in the city. It is easily infected by the anthracnose fungus, which causes its leaves to turn brown. Almost all butcher blocks are made of sycamore because the wood is tough, hard, and difficult to split. The name *occidentalis* is Latin for western.

Hardiness: Zones 4-9

Tree of Heaven/Ailanthus; *Ailanthus altissima* (ay-LAN-thus al-TISS-sim-muh)

A native of China, the tree of heaven is a fast-growing, tall tree that can, because of its palmlike compound leaves, look tropical. The multitudes of seeds that grow on the female trees germinate easily, resulting in dozens of unwanted seedlings. As a result, this tree has become an urban weed tree. Because of its rapid growth rate, however, it has been used for erosion control in places where few other trees can survive. The tree has pale, weak wood, not good for much other than paper pulp.

Hardiness: Zones 4-8 (not common in the South)

Tuliptree/Yellow Poplar; *Liriodendron tulipfera* (leer-e-o-DEN-dron too-lip-IF-er-uh)

The tuliptree is the state tree of Indiana, Kentucky, and Tennessee, largely because it was an important tree in the early days of settlement. Tuliptrees have tall, straight trunks and very hard wood, making them well suited for railroad ties and fence posts. Daniel Boone used a tuliptree for his 60-foot dugout canoe.

Hardiness: Zones 4-9

Tupelo, Black/Blackgum; *Nyssa sylvatica* (NISS-uh sill-VAT-ih-kuh)

Bees love this tree, and it is one of the best honey-producing trees in North America. Horticulturalist Michael Dirr calls it "one of our most beautiful native trees . . . [with] outstanding summer and fall foliage." It was named Urban Tree of the Year in 2008 partly because of its "smorgasbord of yellow to orange to scarlet leaves" in autumn. The tree has rich, green foliage in summer; interesting, alligatorlike bark; and a graceful, bare winter form. Its fruits are quickly eaten by birds, leaving little mess.

Hardiness: Zones 4-9

Walnut, Black; *Juglans nigra* (JOO-glanz NYE-gruh)

The scientific name *juglans* is a contraction of two Latin words and means "nut of Jupiter." *Nigra* means "black" and refers to the black bark and nuts. Native Americans and early settlers once used the tree for food, black dye and ink, medicine, fence posts, and furniture. Today, walnuts from this beautiful tree are used in many foods (including brownies and ice cream), while black walnut wood is highly prized for fine furniture and paneling.

Hardiness: Zones 4-9

Willow, Black; *Salix nigra* (SAY-lix NYE-gruh)

The wood of the black willow tree is used for boxes and crates, barn floors, packing cases, tabletops, wooden novelties, polo balls, charcoal, and pulp. In the past, it's been used to make artificial limbs because it's lightweight and doesn't splinter easily.

Hardiness: Zones 4-8

Willow, Weeping/Golden Weeping Willow; *Salix alba* 'Vitellina' (SAY-lix AL-buh)

This cultivar of willow was developed about 1620 in Switzerland. It is now common in North America. When mature, the tree is distinctive, with long, drooping branches reaching nearly to the ground. Horticulturalist Michael Dirr calls this tree "rather dignified and majestic." It does best in moist soils.

Hardiness: Zones 2-8 (9)

Yellowwood; *Cladrastis kentukea* (kluh-DRASS-tiss ken-TUCK-ee-uh)

Yellowwood is an excellent tree with fragrant flowers and interesting foliage, but it is not a common tree in town or in the woods. Interestingly, there is a state forest in Brown County, Indiana, named after this tree. The name comes from the tree's bright, yellow wood, which is a source of yellow dye.

Hardiness: Zones 4-8

Yew; *Taxus (species)* (TAK-suss)

Yews are evergreens that may be shrubs or small trees. They are extremely popular as foundation plantings around homes and public buildings. The scientific name comes from the Greek word for yew, *taxos,* and perhaps also from *taxon,* meaning "bow"—yew wood is used to make bows. Many of the yews for sale today are *Taxus cuspidate,* a native of Japan, or *Taxus x media,* a hybrid yew.

Hardiness: Zones 4-7

Zelkova, Japanese; *Zelkova serrata* (zel-KOE-vuh sair-AY-tuh)

Japanese zelkova is in the same family as the American elm and similarly grows into a large, vase-shaped tree. It is resistant to Dutch elm disease. Because zelkova wood is strong and has a beautiful grain, it is sometimes used for making furniture. *Serrata* means "sawtoothed" or "serrated."

Hardiness: Zones 5-8

Glossary

Alternate. An arrangement of leaves on a twig in which the leaves are not attached in pairs but instead are attached singly, usually on alternating sides of the twig.

Apex. The tip of a leaf blade—at the opposite end from the base.

Base. The part of a leaf blade where it attaches to the leafstalk.

Bipinnate. A type of compound leaf in which the center stalk branches into side stalks that then bear leaflets (e.g. Kentucky coffeetree).

Blade. The flat part of a leaf (or leaflet if compound), not including the leafstalk.

Bract. A leaflike structure usually located behind a flower. Bracts are usually green, although the bracts behind the flowering dogwood blossom are white and look like petals.

Bud. A structure on a twig that contains an unopened flower or leaf.

Capsule. A dry fruit that splits open to release its seeds (e.g. the fruit of a cottonwood tree).

Catkin. A long, narrow, caterpillarlike structure composed of many tiny flowers, which usually have either stamens or pistils, seldom both.

Chlorophyll. The chemical that is necessary for photosynthesis (the production of sugar) in leaves and gives leaves their green color.

Compound leaf. A leaf composed of three or more blades (each called leaflets).

Cone. A roughly conical structure with often woody or papery scales that opens when mature and releases seeds. Found on conifers (such as pines, spruces, and firs).

Conifer. Tree whose seeds form in cones (such as pine, spruce, or fir trees).

Cultivar. A "cultivated variety" of a tree or other plant bred to maintain a specific characteristic or set of characteristics.

Deciduous. Plants that drop their leaves every autumn. A few deciduous trees, such as oaks, hold on to some of their dead leaves through much of the winter, dropping them before new growth occurs in spring.

Double serrated or **double toothed.** Leaves whose edges have large and small teeth together.

Evergreen tree. Tree whose leaves remain for several growing seasons.

Flower. The reproductive structure of a plant that contains either a stamen (which produces pollen) or a pistil (which, after fertilization, produces seeds) or both.

Fruit. The part of a plant in which seeds are grown or contained.

Hardiness. The ability of a plant to withstand temperature extremes.

Hardiness zone. A geographical region of North America as seen on the USDA Plant Hardiness Zone Map that has a specific average annual coldest temperature.

Hybrid. A tree with parentage that includes two different species (e.g. common apple or London planetree).

Key. A dry, winged fruit (e.g. ash or a single maple fruit).

Lateral vein. One of the many veins that extend out from the midrib of a leaf.

Leaf. The "food factories" of a plant; the part of a plant where water and carbon dioxide are chemically combined in a process called photosynthesis to form sugar and oxygen. A flat leaf is composed of a blade and leafstalk (or petiole).

Leaf scar. The marking on a twig visible when a leaf is removed.

Leaflet. One of the several blades that make up a compound leaf.

Leafstalk. The structure that connects a leaf blade to a woody twig or shoot. The base is usually enlarged where it comes in contact with a bud.

Lenticel. A bump or narrow horizontal structure on the bark of some trees that allows air to pass into and out of the branch.

Lobe. A part of a leaf blade that extends out from the rest of the blade (such as the extensions on a maple leaf).

Margin. The edges of a leaf blade.

Midrib. The center or middle vein of a leaf.

Needle. A leaf that is long and very narrow, like a sewing needle (e.g. pine or spruce needles). Some needles are flat (e.g. yew needles). Most needles are evergreen.

Opposite. An arrangement of leaves on a twig in which the leaves are attached in pairs, one on each side of the twig.

Ornamental tree. A tree planted because of its attractive structure, flowers, fruits, or leaves.

Palmate. On leaves: 1. A type of compound leaf where all the leaflets are attached to the leafstalk at the same place (e.g. Ohio buckeye). The leaflets then radiate outward from the center (much as fingers all extend from the palm of a hand); 2. A pattern of lobes that all extend from the base of a leaf (e.g. maple); 3. A pattern of veins of a leaf whereby at least 5 main veins all extend from the base of the leaf (e.g. maple or redbud).

Petiole. The botanical term for a leafstalk.

Phloem. Structures in the inner bark that transport sugary sap made in the leaves downward toward the roots.

Photosynthesis. The chemical process that occurs within leaves whereby light energy converts water and carbon dioxide into sugar and oxygen.

Pinnnate. On leaves: 1. A type of compound leaf where all the leaflets are attached to an extension of the leafstalk in two rows like the hairs on a feather, with one row on each side (e.g. ash); 2. A featherlike pattern of lobes that extend outward on (usually) both sides of the center vein (e.g. white oak); 3. A featherlike pattern of veins whereby the major lateral veins are connected along length of the center vein (e.g. elm).

Pistil. The structure within a flower, which, after fertilization, produces seeds. Not all flowers have pistils.

Pod. A long, usually dry fruit (like a pea pod) such as those on the honeylocust and catalpa trees.

Pressing leaves. The process of keeping leaves flat until they dry.

Roots. The parts of a plant (usually underground) that absorb the water and dissolved minerals needed by the plant.

Samara. A dry, thin, flat fruit that contains 1 seed, such as those on maple, ash, and elm trees.

Scales. 1. Tiny, overlapping leaves of certain conifers (such as arborvitae); 2. The overlapping woody or papery segments of a cone.

Scientific name. The Latin or Latinized name of a tree or other living organism, composed of a genus name and a descriptor. Together, the two words become the name of a species. While there may be many common names of a tree, there is only one scientific name. Scientific names are always written in italics.

Serrated leaf. A leaf with a toothed margin where the teeth point toward the tip.

Shrub. A woody perennial plant, usually with many stems instead of one trunk, that seldom reaches a height of 10 feet.

Simple leaf. A leaf with 1 blade.

Sinus. The space between two lobes on a leaf.

Species. A group of similar plants that freely reproduce among each other.

Stamen. The structure within a flower that produces pollen. Not all flowers have stamens.

Subopposite. An arrangement of leaves on a twig in which the leaves are attached in pairs very close to, but not exactly opposite, each other.

Taproot. A large, central root generally growing straight downward.

Tree. A perennial plant, 10 feet or higher at maturity, with a woody trunk (usually just one), branches, and twigs supporting a crown of leaves.

Trunk. The base stem of a tree.

Urban forest. The trees growing in a city or town.

USDA. United States Department of Agriculture.

Variety. Trees of a particular species that have specific characteristics different from other trees in that species.

Whorled. An arrangement of 3 or more leaves that are attached from a single place on the twig.

Xylem. Sapwood. Structures of the trunk or branches of a tree that transport water and dissolved minerals from the roots to the leaves. Tree leaves are the remains of old xylem tissue.

References

PRINT SOURCES

Arnold, Henry F. *Trees in Urban Design.* Van Nostrand Reinhold: New York, 1931.

Buckstrup, M. "Presenting the 2007 SMA Tree of the Year: Baldcypress." *City Trees,* January/February 2007.

Buckstrup, M. "Presenting the 2009 SMA Tree of the Year: Chinkapin Oak." *City Trees,* January/February 2009.

Cassens, Daniel L., Eva Haviarova, and Sally Weeks. *Wood from Midwestern Trees.* Department of Forestry and Natural Resources, Purdue University: West Lafayette, IN, 2007.

Daniels, Roland. *Street Trees.* College of Agriculture, The Pennsylvania State University: University Park, PA, 1975.

Dirr, Michael A. *Manual of Woody Landscape Plants: Their Identification, Ornamental Characteristics, Culture, Propagation, and Uses.* Fifth Edition. Stipes Publishing L.L.D.: Champaign, IL, 1998.

Farrar, John Laird. *Trees of the Northern United States and Canada.* Iowa State University Press: Ames, IA, 1995.

Gallob, Edward. *City Leaves, City Trees.* Charles Scribner's Sons: New York, 1972.

Gilman, Edward F., and Dennis G. Watson. Fact Sheets. Environmental Horticulture Department, Florida Cooperative Extension Service, Revised by the Forest Service, U.S. Department of Agriculture: Washington, D.C., 1993–94.

Gould, H. P. *Peach-growing.* The Macmillan Company: New York, 1918.

Grimm, William C. *The Book of Trees.* The Stackpole Company: Harrisburg, PA, 1962.

Jablonski, Eike. "Oaks: An Overview." *Tag Along,* Fall 2005, Vol 4, No. 3. Taltree Arboretum: Valparaiso, IN.

Jackson, Marion T. *101 Trees of Indiana.* Indiana University Press: Bloomington and Indianapolis, IN, 2004.

Jacobson, Arthur Lee. *North American Landscape Trees.* Ten Speed Press: Berkeley, CA, 1996.

Janick, J., and R. E. Paull, eds. *The Encyclopedia of Fruit and Nuts.* Oxford University Press: New York, 2008.

Layne, D. R., and Daniele Bassi. *The Peach: Botany, Production, and Uses.* CAB International: Wallingford, Oxfordshire, UK, 2008.

Nadel, Ira Bruce, Cornelia Hahn Oberlander, and Lesley R. Bohm. *Trees in the City.* Pergamon Press: New York, 1977.

Peattie, Donald Culross. *A Natural History of Trees of Eastern and Central North America.* Houghton Mifflin: Boston, 1950.

Peper, Paula J., E. Gregory McPherson, James R. Simpson, Kelaine E. Vargas, and Qingfu Xiao. *Lower Midwest Community Tree Guide: Benefits, Costs, and Strategic Planting.* United States Department of Agriculture: Washington, D.C. 2009.

Plotnik, Arthur. *The Urban Tree Book: An Uncommon Field Guide for City and Town.* Three Rivers Press: New York, 2000.

Rodd, Tony, and Jennifer Stackhouse. *Trees: A Visual Guide.* University of California Press: Berkeley and Los Angeles, 2008.

Schoon, K. J. "The Midwest Trban Tree Index." Journal of Arboriculture, 1993, 19 (4), 230–237.

Sharp, Joellen, Jo Ellen Meyers, and Tom Tyler. *The Indiana Gardener's Guide.* Coolspring Press: Franklin, Tennessee, 2003.

Shores, John Blake. "SMA Selects the 2011 Urban Tree of the Year: Goldenraintree." *City Trees,* January/February 2011, Vol 47 (1).

Sibley, David Allen. *The Sibley Guide to Trees.* Alfred A. Knopf: New York, 2009.

Sivyer, D. "Presenting the 2008 Tree of the Year: Nyssa Sylvatica." *City Trees,* January/February 2008.

United States Department of Agriculture. Publication No. 1475. Washington, DC, 1990.

United States Department of Commerce, Bureau of the Census. *Census and You.* Washington, DC, February 1993.

Weeks, Sally S. *Red and White Mulberry in Indiana.* Forestry and Natural Resources. Purdue University: West Lafayette, IN, 2003.

Williams, Michael D. *Identifying Trees: An All-Season Guide to Eastern North America.* Stackpole Books: Mechanicsburg, PA, 2007.

ONLINE SOURCES

About.com: Canada Online, Provincial Trees of Canada: canadaonline.about.com/library/bl/blprovtrees.htm.

Arbor Day Foundation, Arborday.org Tree Guide: www.arborday.org/trees/treeGuide/index.cfm.

Bernheim Arboretem: www.bernheim.org.

Brand, Mark, UConn Plant Database, University of Connecticut: www.hort.uconn.edu/Plants/index.html.

Canadian Food Inspection Agency: www.inspection.gc.ca/english/plaveg/pestrava/agrpla/agrplae.shtml.

Canadian Forest Service: cfs.nrcan.gc.ca.

Center for New Crops & Plant Products, Purdue University, West Lafayette, IN: www.hort.purdue.edu/newcrop/default.html.

Floridata Plant Browser. www.floridata.com/FloridataBase/browseFloridata.cfm.

Nix, Steve. "Using Anatomy and Habitat to Identify a Tree." About.com Guide to Forestry: forestry.about.com/od/thecompletetree/u/tree_anatomy.htm.

Kentucky Department for Libraries and Archives: Kentucky State Tree: www.kdla.ky.gov/resources/kytree.htm#CoffeeTree.

Ladd Arboretum and Nature Center: http://laddarboretum.org/.

Michigan State University, "Emerald Ash Borer": www.emeraldashborer.info/.

Montreal Botanical Garden: www2.ville.montreal.qc.ca/jardin/en/menu.htm.

National Park Service, "Cherry Blossom Festival": www.nps.gov/cherry/cherry-blossom-history.htm.

Nebraska Forest Service: www.nfs.unl.edu/.

Ohio DNR Division of Forestry: http://www.dnr.state.oh.us/tabid/5343/Default.aspx.

Ohio Public Library Network: www.oplin.org/tree/.

The Ohio State University, Horticulture and Crop Science: www.hcs.ohio-state.edu.

Plant Conservation Alliance: www.nps.gov/plants/ALIEN/fact/pdf/poal1.pdf.

Purdue University, Horticulture and Landscape Architecture: www.hort.purdue.edu

Steven Foster Group, Inc.: http://stevenfoster.com/education/monograph/hawthorn.html.

United States Department of Agriculture Forest Service: www.na.fs.fed.us.

United States Department of Agriculture Forest Service, "Forest Health Protection-Dutch Elm Disease": www.na.fs.fed.us/fhp/ded/.

United States Department of Agriculture Natural Resources Conservation Service: Plants Database: http://plants.usda.gov.

United States Department of the Interior, National Park Service: www.nps.gov/index.htm.

University of Arkansas Cooperative Extension Service, "Arkansas Tree Identification": www.aragriculture.org/horticulture/trees/default.htm.

University of Connecticut, Horticulture: www.hort.uconn.edu

University of Connecticut Plant Database: http://www.hort.uconn.edu/Plants/index.html.

University of Florida, Institute of Food and Agricultural Sciences: www.sfrc.ufl.edu/4h/

University of Florida, "Southern Trees Fact Sheets": http://edis.ifas.ufl.edu/department_envhort-trees.

University of Wisconsin, Department of Horticulture: www.hort.wisc.edu/master gardener/features/woodies/abmaple/abmaple.htm.

Species Index

Index of Leaf Descriptions

SIMPLE, LOBED LEAVES

COMPOUND LEAVES

RED OR PURPLE SUMMER LEAVES